BIAS IN THE BOOTH

BIAS IN THE BOOTH

AN INSIDER EXPOSES HOW SPORTS MEDIA DISTORT THE NEWS

DYLAN GWINN

REGNERY
PUBLISHING

A Salem Communications Company

Regnery® is a registered trademark of Salem Communications Holding Corporation

Cataloging-in-Publication data on file with the Library of Congress

ISBN 978-1-62157-331-9

Published in the United States by
Regnery Publishing
A Salem Communications Company
300 New Jersey Ave NW
Washington, DC 20001
www.Regnery.com

Distributed to the trade by
Perseus Distribution
250 West 57th Street
New York, NY 10107

Manufactured in the United States of America

10 9 8 7 6 5 4 3 2 1

Books are available in quantity for promotional or premium use. For information on discounts and terms, please visit our website: www. Regnery.com.

For my parents, Bruce and Vinia Gwinn

CONTENTS

INTRODUCTION

Sometimes it's easier to say what a book is not, as opposed to saying what it actually is. So, let's start there. What you're holding in your hand right now is not a book about sports. Nor is it a traditional book about the sports media where I catalogue and detail a career spent covering and writing about the biggest stars in sports and blah, blah, blah, blah.

No, what you're holding in your hand is something altogether different. This is a book about how virtually the entire sports media have been overrun with liberal activists trying to implement and advance their liberal agenda.

I've been watching sports for most of my life. Being that I've made a career in sports talk radio, I've probably watched a lot more sports than is healthy or advisable. Like many of you, I remember a time when people flocked to sports because they were fun and entertaining, even awe-inspiring at their best, and an escape from the BS and politically correct hysteria of the "real world."

Political news and commentary were something you didn't often find in sports, because they were contentious and harsh, a serious business where the burdens of the real world were hung around your neck. Sports were an oasis, a safe zone, that one place where you could shut out all the frustrations and nonsense and seriousness of life and morph into an overgrown, screaming, jumping, foam-finger-waving thirteen-year-old.

Now that former "safe zone" has become a political crazy zone, as broadcasters, writers, and TV personalities who are supposed to be talking about Peyton Manning and Tom Brady, Bryce Harper and Justin Verlander, Dwight Howard and Kevin Love, wax silly on everything from religion and politics to homosexuality, rape, race-baiting, and every other form of progressive nuttiness you can imagine. We're fast approaching a point where there's going to be no real difference between Bob Costas and Rachel Maddow. Except one of them is a man. I think.

Not that the sports media's leftward slouch wasn't always there. I always knew the sports media were liberal. But their liberalism was tempered by the fact that their primary job was sports, and that's where they needed to focus their attention. I could deal with the occasional politically correct quip from Bob Costas as long as it was only occasional and the sports-to-politics balance was heavily tilted toward sports.

But nowadays that scale is about as balanced as a tilt-a-whirl. Politics—and the sports media's desire to advance a political agenda—now determine what stories get covered. Meet, for instance, seventh-round draft pick Michael Sam, an otherwise unremarkable player cut from the final roster of the team that drafted him, not signed onto their practice squad, and yet a headliner in the sports media for months, all because the liberal media have adopted certain sexual practices as worthy of a crusade.

In the spirit of saying what this book is not, I wish to make clear that I have no desire for the sports media to be conservative either. I'm not writing this book because I want to shift their ideology and worldview from liberal to conservative. I'm writing this book because I want the sports media to talk about sports, not politics. In short, I want the sports media to do their job.

But the inescapable fact of the matter is that the sports media, along with the mainstream media, have become just another font of liberal activism. A decade and a half ago, former Emmy Award–winning CBS journalist (and a correspondent for HBO's *Real Sports with Bryant Gumbel*) Bernard Goldberg wrote a classic number one *New York Times* bestseller about American journalism called *Bias*. Goldberg at the time was a liberal himself, but he was appalled at the casual yet pervasive bias of his mainstream media colleagues who weren't interested in simply reporting the facts, or even telling the truth, but were focused on advancing a left-wing agenda, often without even thinking about it, so deeply ingrained was their bias. He thought that was unprofessional—and he was right.

In sports, the stakes might be smaller, but in some ways the offense is even worse. Fans have a right to enjoy a game, or a discussion of sports topics, without feeling like they're being put through a social indoctrination regimen, especially a social indoctrination program that's run by people whose sole accomplishment in life is that they can remember who hit cleanup for the Big Red Machine in the seventies. (Side note: it was Johnny Bench.) And that's part of the problem too. Many sports reporters and commentators recognize that they deal in trivialities, and yet they want to make a bigger impact on society, they want to feel more important, they want to inflate their egos by lecturing you, and as a consequence they often do their real jobs not very well. This book is for all of us who find ourselves wanting to shout, "Shut up and give me the box score!"

CHAPTER ONE

LANDING ON TRAYVON

Radio is an industry dominated by white people. In all honesty, it looks an awful lot like a Mumford & Sons concert in there: shaggy beards and ill-fitting jeans mixed with a healthy dose of malnutrition and metrosexuality. You know the types. Yet one day in early 2012, I sat show-prepping in the newsroom, sitting with a black producer and a black intern. Eventually our discussion turned to a story that had dwarfed all other news: Trayvon Martin and George Zimmerman.

The headlines were that the local prosecutors would not charge George Zimmerman with Trayvon Martin's murder. This greatly upset the producer and the intern. But then our conversation turned to the sports community.

PRODUCER: I just wish somebody would stand up and do something. Like maybe a Florida team; if they would just make a statement it would bring the kind of attention this deserves.

INTERN: Oh absolutely. But nobody probably will.

ME: Why do you want that? How is it the job of a sports team, or a sports league, to get involved in a murder trial?

PRODUCER: Because this isn't just a murder trial. This is a racial murder trial.

ME: So in other words, it's not about Trayvon Martin, it's about George Zimmerman?

PRODUCER: No, it's not all because of that …

ME: But how many black kids are killed in South Florida every year by other black kids? Probably hundreds. Yet you're not asking a Florida team to make a stand over any of them. You're asking a Florida team to make a stand here because of who the murderer is. Not because of the kid who got murdered.

Now, I'm sure you're asking yourselves: *But, Dylan! What the heck are you doing?!? Why bring up Trayvon Martin? I thought this was a book about sports media.* Relax, this is a book about sports media. And no, Trayvon Martin's story should never have been a sports media story. But it was, because sports media, and athletes, made it into a story that had to do with sports.

Trayvon Martin didn't land on us; we decided to land on Trayvon Martin. And when the liberal sports media land on a topic of which they have virtually no knowledge, and very little understanding, it makes a really bad sound … kind of like Nickelback, but racist. Now, I bring up the discussion I had at the radio station for several reasons.

First of all, I had a good relationship with this producer; we could be honest with each other, and though our conversation about Trayvon became contentious at times, it didn't end badly. Second, I want to give him credit for basically predicting the Miami Heat "hoodie photo" that they would release only a couple of months later.

But most of all I want to illustrate the fact that *plenty* of people in the "social justice"–driven, liberal sports media *wanted* to land on the Trayvon Martin story in any way they could and found any excuse they could to do it. Similar discussions occurred at radio and television sports desks all over the country despite the fact that this story had absolutely nothing to do with sports.

How do I know this? Because in April 2012, thirteen members of the Miami Heat donned hoodies, just as Trayvon had been wearing when he was shot, for a group photo to show solidarity and put forth the idea that any of them could have been the victim. Then immediately after the "hoodie photo" went viral, the sports media went apoplectic. Michael Wallace, writing in the *Miami Heat Index* at ESPN.com, applauded the Heat for "standing tall" for Trayvon and explained why the Heat felt they had to do this:

> But this case hits especially close to home for the Heat on several levels. Martin was from Miami Gardens, a community that borders on neighborhoods where Heat players James Jones and Udonis Haslem were raised.... In many ways, this was a civic duty for Wade, James and their teammates.... Like Wade, LeBron also is the father of two young sons. And also like Wade, LeBron grew up in an impoverished area where young black men were more likely to become fatal statistics than phenoms in the field of sports.[1]

A civic duty, huh? Funny how this civic duty only kicks in when someone of a lighter complexion pulls the trigger. In August 2013, in that very same Miami Gardens neighborhood, twelve-year-old Tequila Forshee was killed by stray bullets as she sat in her family's living room having her hair braided.[2] An innocent little girl, with her whole life ahead of her, snuffed out like she was nothing by stray bullets fired by some shred of human excrement I sincerely hope is somebody's prison wife right now. But you've never heard of Tequila Forshee before. Why?

Why didn't this sense of "civic duty" kick in for her? After all, she was from Udonis Haslem and James Jones's old neighborhood; yet no players "stood tall" for Tequila. No members of the Heat braided their hair for her. Maybe it's because her killer wasn't white. In which case, apparently, there's no point "standing tall." Make sense? If it does, you're an idiot.

Michael Wallace is no doubt right when he says that young black men from impoverished areas are far "more likely to become fatal statistics than phenoms in the field of sports." But what he left out is that they're far more likely to become fatal statistics *at the hands of other black men* than they are by idiot, vigilante neighborhood-watch types. The fact is, according to the Bureau of Justice Statistics of the U.S. Department of Justice, about 93 percent of black murder victims are murdered by other blacks; and blacks, who are about 13 percent of the population, commit more than half of all American homicides.[3]

So is there a crime problem in black America? Yes—and if the Miami Heat or any other players wanted to do something about it, donning hoodies in solidarity with Trayvon was about the least effective thing they could have done.

But for sports media, grandstanding is just fine. Sports columnist David Hyde, in the *Sun Sentinel*, lamented how "over the past few decades," before the Heat made their brave stand for Trayvon, "the model of the sports hero shrank." He continued:

> It didn't start with Tiger Woods' refusal to say something—anything—about the lack of black members at certain country clubs or of women at Augusta National. It didn't start with Michael Jordan's avoiding political conversations because, as the namesake of the Air Jordan sneaker famously said, "Republicans buy shoes too." It's a cultural slide we've all participated in—athletes, media and fans—of expecting players only to play great and never to think great like Arthur Ashe, prod great like Muhammad Ali, talk great like Billie Jean King or Martina Navratilova, or challenge in a great way like Jim Brown or Oscar Robertson.[4]

Maybe we only care about players playing great because that's the only reason why we watch them. Tom Brady is a phenomenal quarterback. That's what he does, and that's what he knows. If I wanted to learn how to read a zone-dog blitz, I'd go to Brady. If I wanted insight on political unrest in Ukraine, or crop production in Malaysia, I'd go to somebody else. It's not that I don't expect my athletes to "think great"; I would just prefer they keep those "great" thoughts to themselves, because I don't watch them for that. Nor is it the shrinking of the "sports hero"; if anything, athletes are more famous and wealthy today than they've ever been. What it is (big-word alert) is the compartmentalization of the world. I don't need a political Muhammad Ali in my life; if I want to watch an anti-American Muslim scream about the injustices perpetrated by America, I can watch MSNBC. I don't need Billie Jean King to tell me what it's like to be gay; I have HBO and *Modern Family* for that. Back when Muhammad Ali and Billie Jean King were around, there were three television stations and five major national newspapers. Now we have cable channels that cover everything from underwater basket-weaving to lesbian biker gangs, and we have podcasts, blogs, satellite radio, terrestrial radio, apps, tweets, and websites with wannabe experts galore. What I want, *and what I think most people want,* is for their athletes to entertain them with the grace, skill, and power of their sport, and to provide an escape from all the real-world stuff that we have to deal with on a daily basis. Almost every sports fan wants sports to be a politics-free zone, and our job as media isn't to insert realism into people's escapism. And sports media should serve the sports fans, not push the commentators' political agendas, and not push athletes to make political statements (and they're always pushing in one direction, in case you didn't notice).

That said, Hyde's contention that today's athletes lack political activism is a joke. Michael Jordan, whom Hyde disses for avoiding "political conversations," was one of Barack Obama's most significant private campaign donors. In fact, Jordan, along with then–NBA commissioner David Stern, hosted a massive campaign fund-raising dinner for Obama in New York City right before the 2012 election called the "Obama Classic." The event attracted multiple NBA players, including Kyrie Irving, John Wall, Harrison Barnes, Austin Rivers, and many others. Jordan himself, whose financial support of Obama goes back as far as his Senate run in 2004, has raised and donated millions to Obama. What annoys leftist sports writers like David Hyde is the lack of 1960s– and 1970s–era photo-ops: no raised fists, no burning bras, no public protests. The hoodie photo brought back, for the leftist sport media, the good old days.

But for athletes the "movement" has grown more sophisticated as it has grown more corporate. For many years "the Benjamins" have flown out of athletes' wallets and into the coffers of leftist politicians in copious amounts. The $5,000-a-plate dinner *is* the new burning bra. But that, of course, doesn't make for good copy or commentary of the sort that Benjamin Hochman of the *Denver Post* could turn out praising LeBron James and the Heat for the hoodie photo:

> Ever since [LeBron] made "take my talents" a punch line, ever since he floundered in NBA Finals news conferences as if he were Captain Queeg, ever since he forgot about his fans and where he came from, basketball's best player has become a PR nightmare. Your mouth opens when he plays, and your mouth opens when he opens his mouth. But LeBron James did something positive this past week with his public platform.
>
> The killing has sparked a debate about racial profiling. So James posted a photo on his Twitter account (he has more than 4 million followers). The photo featured the Miami Heat players all wearing sweat shirt hoods over their heads. Using hash tags to provide commentary, James wrote: #WeAreTrayvonMartin #Hoodies #Stereotyped #WeWantJustice.[5]

In fact, you would have had to look very hard to find any criticism of what the Heat had done. The so-called great fear of the NBA, that its majority fan demographic of suburban whites would be put off by the political stance of its players, mostly urban and black, seemed not to materialize at all. Virtually the entire sports world, fans included, either stood in full-throated support or stayed ambivalent about what the Heat had done in taking the "hoodie photo." Yet the media, in their zest to reward the Heat for the kind of activism they wanted to see more of, continued to heap on the praise. Jason Whitlock, then of Fox Sports, spoke of "courage" in what the team had done:

> Courage can be every bit as contagious as cowardice. Wade and James spread the courage virus throughout the NBA on Friday. At the formation of Miami's "Big Three," James and his defenders claimed the establishment was threatened by young black athletes seizing their power and using it.
>
> For the first time, I now believe James understands his power. And it wasn't in forcing NBA executives to come to his hometown, Akron, Ohio, to grovel at his feet, or announcing his relocation to South Beach on national TV or thumbing his nose at Dan Gilbert as he left Cleveland.
>
> LeBron's power is in using his platform, when appropriate, to make the establishment stretch beyond its comfort zone when it comes to dealing with the powerless. LeBron's heart has always been in the right place. Teaming with Wade, a near equal in terms of talent and a big brother in terms of maturity, has moved LeBron's head where his heart is.[6]

How much "courage" is truly involved in tweeting out a pic that garners universal praise? On the contrary, something much more courageous came later from Charles Barkley when he announced his agreement with the eventual acquittal of George Zimmerman. *That* took incredible balls.

Pay close attention to the language Whitlock uses to describe the "power" that LeBron James has, and needs to use, *"when appropriate, to make the establishment stretch beyond its comfort zone when it comes to dealing with the powerless* [emphasis added]." So this is the role of the best player in the NBA? To make the establishment "stretch" for the "powerless"? Whitlock is, allegedly, a sports writer, but he could just as easily be writing a sports version of Saul Alinsky's *Rules for Radicals*. What Whitlock really means is that he wants LeBron and other high-profile black athletes to become activists for leftist political causes.

To the sports media, Nike ads, McDonald's commercials, appearances at Boys and Girls Clubs, even campaign contributions, are a waste of the power of someone like LeBron James. Don't believe me? Here's former NBA player Etan Thomas writing in the *Washington Post* about the "Obama Classic," and more specifically about the "wasted power" of Michael Jordan:

> In a recent article on ESPN, LZ Granderson reminds us of Jordan's infamous "Republicans buy sneakers, too" comment that has become the prime example of the overall tragedy of *wasted power* [emphasis added]. Jordan reportedly made the comment when declining to endorse black Democrat Harvey Gantt in a North Carolina 1990 Senate race against Jessie Helms (R).
>
> Jordan had the ability to influence an entire generation of young people especially within the black community. But instead he chose to remain publicly neutral in all matters racial and political. He never capitalized on his potential to mobilize the black community on social issues. Simply put, he never wanted to continue the work of the great Muhammad Ali and Jim Brown, both politically outspoken athletes. As his support for President Obama shows, he might have changed his tune.[7]

Etan Thomas and his fellow leftists in sports media think it's not enough for great athletes to inspire kids to work hard and try to excel in sports and in life. No, they should use their wealth and their fame to "mobilize the black community on social issues." Translation: get them to vote Democrat or get them to the picket lines, and make sure they do and say the right things when they're there.

When LeBron James left Cleveland for Miami, his former employer Dan Gilbert wrote a childish hit piece attacking him. At the time many black people, including Jesse Jackson and Marc Lamont Hill, a CNN commentator, accused Gilbert of having a "slave master" mentality toward his players, acting as if he "owned" them.[8]

Gilbert and LeBron have since made up, but the idea that multi-million-dollar black athletes are slaves is a theory as absurd as it is prevalent. Etan Thomas wrote in the *Washington Post*:

> The [early, apolitical] stance that Jordan's behavior illustrated was referenced in William Rhoden's book, "40 Million Dollar Slaves: The Rise, Fall and Redemption of Black Athletes," in which the author said: "Isolated and alienated from their native networks and increasingly cloistered into new networks as they become corporatized entities, they are excised from their communities as they fulfill their professional responsibilities and disconnected from the networks of people, in many cases predominately African-American, who once comprised their 'community.' This leads to a general ignorance of the issues impacting a vast majority of African-Americans across the country."[9]

Translation: As black athletes become more successful, they become less "black." And just as troubling for activists, as black athletes become more successful, the harder they are to control and to manipulate.

To the activists, black athletes should all think alike. They should all think like *them*. No old plantation slave master could control the thoughts of his slaves, but the new, liberal, "progressive" activists in the sports media think we all, but blacks especially, have to think alike. If you think for yourself, you're selling out.

The activists' message to young black athletes is that if they work hard and succeed, they'll be held in corporate bondage to some billionaire owner who will alienate them from their "community." What an awesome message! What a way to encourage the kids! Being black is somehow antipathetic to success...unless you become politically active in left-wing causes. Then, your "blackness" will be enshrined forever.

What really bothers the likes of William Rhoden and Etan Thomas is not that these athletes are "slaves," but that they're not slaves *to them*. They're upset that they can't just pick up the phone and tell Tiger Woods to start spouting whatever leftist drivel they need spouted, to be the "voice" of Jason Whitlock's "powerless." That's why the leftist sports media made their collective O-face after the Miami Heat's hoodie photo. It had nothing to do with Trayvon Martin. None of it did. To them, it was a symbol that the era of the "forty-million-dollar slave" might be coming to an end; a sign that ultra-successful, PR-savvy black athletes might, just might, be willing to step into political controversy, giving leftists an awesomely powerful weapon to wield against the "establishment." And it appears that transformation is now well under way, with LeBron James doing commercials promoting Obamacare. Such statements are "safe" too in the sense that while Obamacare or the Trayvon Martin case are politically controversial, any liberal statements from athletes will be applauded by the liberal (including sports) media.

One of the ironies and tragedies of the Trayvon Martin case is that justice and common sense were shot down with him. The "injustice" of Zimmerman's acquittal was not the result of racism from the establishment, but the result of the establishment's bending over backward to try and assuage the anger represented by the likes of the Heat. George Zimmerman should never have been charged with murder. He called 911, for God's sake. How many murderers, other than in a Monty Python movie, *The Benny Hill Show*, or some kind of bad British comedy skit, actually call the cops?

But if you don't want to hear this from me (a non-lawyer), then hear it from Alan Dershowitz, a Harvard Law professor with impeccable liberal credentials. Here is some of what he had to say in an interview on CNN's *State of the Union* about what went wrong in the Zimmerman trial:

> There was political pressure on the governor, and he appointed somebody [special prosecutor Angela Corey] who had the worst reputation in Florida for overcharging. And she did exactly what she was supposed to do; she overcharged. She charged second-degree murder in a case where there was reasonable doubt written all over it.[10]

In another appearance, on Mike Huckabee's show *Huckabee* on Fox News, Dershowitz detailed how Corey's behavior even "bordered on criminal conduct."

> "She submitted an affidavit that was, if not perjurious, completely misleading. She violated all kinds of rules of the profession," Dershowitz told Huckabee.

"Halfway through the trial she realized she wasn't going to get a second degree murder verdict, so she asked for a compromised verdict, for manslaughter. And then, she went even further and said that she was going to charge him with child abuse and felony murder. That was such a stretch that it goes beyond anything professionally responsible. She was among the most irresponsible prosecutors I've seen in 50 years of litigating cases, and believe me, I've seen good prosecutors, bad prosecutors, but rarely have I seen one as bad as this prosecutor."[11]

The "racism" of the Trayvon Martin case had nothing to do with animosity toward blacks; the "racism" was of a legal system going to absurd lengths to prove that it wasn't racist, bringing a case that should never have been brought.

At the forefront of the mob demanding "justice" for Trayvon Martin were the sports media and more than a few players. The frenzy they and others helped stir up distracted millions of people from the actual facts of the case, encouraged the prosecutor to overreach, and then led to an explosion of outrage on social media after the verdict came down. Roddy White of the Atlanta Falcons tweeted: "All them jurors should go home tonight and kill themselves for letting a grown man get away with killing a kid."[12]

James Harrison, then of the Bengals, weighed in: "Think I'll go pick a fight and get my ass kicked then pull my gun and kill somebody and see if I can get away..."[13]

And Stevie Johnson, then of the Bills, gave us some top-drawer insight as well: "Living in a world where you fight dogs; you could lose everything (Mike Vick)...If you kill a black man you're not guilty! #INjusticeSystem."[14]

Of course, we also live in a world where, if you fight dogs, you can get a $100 million contract after serving your time, but point taken, Stevie. Now, none of this was, or should have been, surprising. Twitter has given a voice to unfiltered and instantaneous commentary from anyone and everyone, and sometimes that works out. Sometimes you get awesomeness. Sometimes you get Roddy White. But what was surprising (though maybe it shouldn't have been) was that even before the verdict, ESPN lifted its long-standing ban on employees expressing political opinions on social media and instead allowed expressions of solidarity with Trayvon Martin.

At first this wasn't the case. On March 23, 2013, the same day that President Obama said, "If I had a son, he'd look like Trayvon," ESPN spokesman Josh Krulewitz affirmed that the network would be enforcing its social-media policy against getting involved in politics: "We completely understand the strong feelings involved. Our decision is in keeping with our long-standing policy for ESPN content. There are other avenues for our people to represent issues outside of sports beyond ESPN Twitter feeds."[15]

But that didn't last long. Only two days later, Krulewitz executed an abrupt about-face: "It's a tragic situation that has led to much thoughtful discussion throughout the company. As a result, in this circumstance, we have decided to allow this particular expression of human sympathy."[16]

Translation: Almost everybody at ESPN's headquarters in Bristol, Connecticut, voted for President Obama, and he's talking about it. Therefore, it's cool. This change in policy led to several ESPN employees donning hoodies on their avatars as signs of support. As Benjamin Chance of Breitbart.com reported, not all were pleased by ESPN's reversal:

The Poynter Institute, the network's former Ombudsman, made clear its disappointment in ESPN's flip-flop: "ESPN's policy that prohibits its commentators, anchors, reporters and analysts from making personal political statements is a good one because it preserves the individual's ability to do powerful work that others cannot do. Although we applaud the willingness to wrestle with the social media policy—it should be a living, breathing document—we were disheartened to see ESPN make an exception to the strongly rooted journalism value of independence."[17]

So was I, because it confirmed that ESPN has *no* "strongly rooted journalism value of independence." It flipped its social-media policy two days after Barack Obama spoke. There's nothing independent about that. And as for journalistic integrity, ESPN has dozens of current and former lawyers on its payroll who could have explained the hopelessness of bringing George Zimmerman to trial on a second-degree murder charge. Those voices were either silent or ignored. The worldwide leader of sports media approached a legal story as a political issue from the start, because that is how they see the world.

So after the Miami Heat's hoodie photo broke the proverbial ice and made it cool for athletes to embrace political issues and social causes, athletes started diving into whatever fashionable current event would get them generous play in the liberal media for "taking a stand." The next flashpoint of silly would be in the NFL.

In late November 2014, shortly after a grand jury in Ferguson, Missouri, decided not to indict white police officer Darren Wilson for fatally shooting a black man named Michael Brown, five members of the St. Louis Rams receiving corps—Tavon Austin, Stedman Bailey,

Kenny Britt, Chris Givens, and Jared Cook—showed their solidarity with Brown and those protesting the grand jury's decision by walking out for opening game introductions in the "hands up, don't shoot" sign of surrender so famously associated with the case.

The gesture was greeted with a mix of cheers and boos inside the stadium, and outside the confines of the ESPN headquarters in Bristol, Connecticut (where the reaction was euphoric), the national reaction was mixed as well. Immediately, questions started circulating about what kind of discipline the NFL and/or the Rams might hand down to the players.

Instead, the NFL decided to issue its own gesture of surrender. In an email response to Yahoo! Sports, NFL vice president of communications Brian McCarthy said, "We respect and understand the concerns of all individuals who have expressed views on this tragic situation."[18]

Rams head coach Jeff Fisher doubled down on the proverbial washing of hands by saying that the players "made the choice to exercise their free speech" and would not be disciplined.[19]

So, in other words, the same league that punishes players for choreographing end-zone celebrations decided to play the free-speech card on a day when five of its players used an NFL broadcast to slam law enforcement and choreograph what amounted to a show of solidarity with the rioters who had taken advantage of the alleged "injustice" of the Ferguson case to loot and burn private property. In fact, that very day, the Rams hosted dozens of Ferguson business owners,[20] or, excuse me, former business owners who had seen their property destroyed by the very people with whom the Rams players had aligned themselves. To the Rams players it was all about race. Charles Barkley, however, had it exactly right when he said that the rioters "aren't real black people"—at least not ones we should admire—but "scumbags." He also laid into the liberal media for misreporting the story in Ferguson because of their racial obsessions and discussed how he had actually read the grand jury testimony that to his mind rightly exonerated the police officer.[21]

The sports media and the NFL, however, were not nearly as thoughtful as Barkley. Indeed, the NFL seemed less worried about the victims of the rioters than about incurring the wrath of angry white hipsters and black radicals and the journalists who love them. For them the issue, allegedly, was free speech.

But the NFL has a funny way of dealing with free speech. In fact, it has a downright nasty habit of only respecting and recognizing speech as free when it's politically convenient for it to do so, and not respecting the speech it does not wish to hear. Such was the case with the Miami Dolphins player Don Jones.[22]

Soon after Michael Sam was drafted and images of him kissing his boyfriend were beamed into living rooms all over the country, Jones took to Twitter and decided to weigh in. He did so by tweeting the following: "OMG" and "Horrible."

A man of few words, clearly. Still, that one word (oh, and the acronym) were enough for Don Jones not only to get fined and suspended, but to have to undergo sensitivity training. But why? What about Don Jones's right to free speech? The Rams players got in front of more than fifty thousand people in the stadium and God knows how many on televisions nationwide to throw gasoline on the still-smoldering flames of racial dysfunction in America, and we were told that all they had done was exercise their right to free speech.

Don Jones tweeted one negative word to 7,500 Twitter followers and was not only fined but sent to get mentally reprogrammed by liberal activists. Why? Because the rioting activists in Ferguson are a protected species to the liberal sports establishment. While those opposed to homosexuality, or at least the visual of two men kissing, are endangered and marked for figurative extinction.

Same thing with Chris Culliver of the San Francisco 49ers. In an interview right before Super Bowl XLVII, Chris Culliver said that gay players wouldn't be welcome on the team.

As quoted in Yahoo! Sports:

> "I don't do the gay guys man," said Culliver, whose Niners play the Baltimore Ravens on Sunday. "I don't do that. No, we don't got no gay people on the team, they gotta get up out of here if they do.
>
> "Can't be with that sweet stuff. Nah … can't be … in the locker room man. Nah."
>
> When quizzed by Lange whether any homosexual athletes would need to keep their sexuality a secret in football, Culliver responded: "Yeah, come out 10 years later after that."[23]

Now, what you don't get from the article is the context of the interview and the way the shock-jock interviewer completely led Culliver into making these comments. In fact, what was really outrageous was what the shock jock, Artie Lange, said, not what Culliver said:

> LANGE: Give me an under/over on white chicks this week?
> CULLIVER: White chicks?
> LANGE: How many are you going to (expletive)?
> CULLIVER: None.
> LANGE: None?
> CULLIVER: I can't (expletive) no white chicks before the Super Bowl.

LANGE: What about gay guys?

CULLIVER: I don't do the gay guys, man. I don't do that.[24]

Somehow, in the great liberal hierarchy of values, saying that you're not into gay guys is worse than treating women as disposable sex toys (actually, it appears that liberals are in favor of that). I'm not saying Culliver doesn't really believe what he said, but when you ask a player how many white women he's going to sleep with that week and then immediately follow that up by asking him if he's been propositioned by any gay guys or would like to have sex with some, well, it gives you an idea of what kind of interview this was. It wasn't like Culliver offered his opinions unsolicited and just started saying inflammatory things.

On the contrary, the whole interview was inflammatory. Lange clearly led Culliver onto the topic and asked the questions in such a way as to get a reaction, which Culliver gave to him, and in a stunning turn that only liberals can do, Lange afterward cast himself as a high and mighty moral judge tut-tutting about how attitudes like Culliver's were unfortunately widespread in the NFL.

To try to stem the ensuing media storm, the 49ers quickly issued a statement: "The San Francisco 49ers reject the comments that were made, and have addressed the matter with Chris. There is no place for discrimination within our organization at any level. We have and always will proudly support the LGBT community."

Culliver issued his own apology. "The derogatory comments I made yesterday were a reflection of thoughts in my head, but they are not how I feel. It has taken me seeing them in print to realize that they are hurtful and ugly. Those discriminating feelings are truly not in my heart. Further, I apologize to those who I have hurt and offended, and I pledge to learn and grow from this experience."

Learning and growing from the experience really meant learning that he wasn't allowed to give an honest answer to a ridiculous question. Where was his right to free speech? Nowhere. Who in the liberal sports media stood up for his right to free speech? Nobody. Because, again, the only speech that is free in the NFL, and that is approved by the liberal sports media, is that which conforms to the marching orders of the activists who have made that once-proud league afraid of its own shadow.

Not that the NFL is alone in that regard, obviously. When LeBron James and Derrick Rose donned "I Can't Breathe" T-shirts in pregame warm-ups in December 2014 to show solidarity with the Eric Garner protestors in New York (Garner had died after a police officer put him in an apparent chokehold in an attempt to arrest him; the officer wasn't indicted), they presented the NBA with the opportunity to prevent its games from turning into the equivalent of a Berkeley campus rally. But again, the league would disappoint. This time it would be NBA commissioner Adam Silver's turn to whiff. In an official statement, Silver said: "I respect Derrick Rose and all of our players for voicing their personal views on important issues, but my preference would be for players to abide by our on-court attire rules."[25]

What a magical tube of weak sauce that is. Silver would have been better off seal-clapping his applause to the players and getting his own "I Can't Breathe" tee as opposed to issuing a statement that made him look completely feckless. Commissioners don't talk about their "preferences" when dealing with players who flagrantly flaunt the league's strict rules about pregame attire. They mete out punishment. Or at least they used to.

This is the same league that fined Jermaine O'Neal $5,000 for wearing his wristband about one inch too high.[26] Yet it does nothing when it comes to players breaking rules to make statements on subjects about eleven billion times more sensitive than where Mr. O'Neal sports his perspiration protection gear.

I wonder if Adam Silver would have waxed poetic about respecting the players for "voicing their personal views" if a bunch of NBA players had shown up to pregames wearing "I Support Traditional Marriage" shirts? Or something really provocative, like a shirt that said, "I Support the Police"? Based on what happened to Chris Culliver and Don Jones, I don't think that would have ended well.

Nor did things end well between George Zimmerman and Trayvon Martin.

For what it's worth, I do blame George Zimmerman for Trayvon Martin's death. Had he stayed in his car and just waited for the cops instead of turning into Paul Blart on 'roids, then Trayvon Martin would likely still be alive today. I don't know anyone who really disputes that. Perhaps if the grossly incompetent prosecutor had initially charged Zimmerman with manslaughter instead of second-degree murder, felony murder, child endangerment, the stock market collapse, the breakup of the Osmonds, and the Hindenburg disaster, then maybe Zimmerman would have been convicted—a verdict I would have supported.

But none of that happened, because Florida's legal and political "establishment" was concerned with shielding itself from charges of racism by placating what it took to be popular opinion. The Trayvon Martin case should never have been a sports story, but once it became one, instead of helping to inform an ill-informed public, the sports media saw a racially charged situation—and lit a match.

CHAPTER TWO

THE SEPARATION OF CHURCH AND SPORT

T he state of Arizona has given us many awesome things: the Grand Canyon, Hoover Dam, Barry Goldwater, Wyatt Earp cleaning up Tombstone, and the great tradition of getting completely tanked and floating down a river. Beer, rubber dinghies, and rivers punctuated by large underwater boulders—what could possibly go wrong? But in the winter of 2014, the Grand Canyon State gave the sports world a collective hernia when its legislature had the audacity to pass SB 1062.

Known as the Religious Freedom Restoration Act, the bill was written primarily in response to an incident in 2006 in which Christian photographers in neighboring New Mexico declined to photograph a gay commitment ceremony (gay weddings were not yet legal), citing conflict with their religious beliefs. The gay couple quickly found another photographer but sued the Christian photographers for allegedly violating their civil rights. The Human Rights Commission of New Mexico and the state courts ruled against the photographers, who appealed all the way to the Supreme Court, which in April 2014 declined to hear the case.

Arizona lawmakers wanted a law that defined and limited when government could intrude on the First Amendment's guarantees of the "free exercise" of religion and freedom of speech to compel people to act against their religious beliefs.

The sports media, faithfully executing their role as distorters of truth, immediately branded the legislation as an "anti-gay bill" and demanded that the NFL pressure Arizona to rescind the law or move the 2015 Super Bowl from Arizona to somewhere else.

One late February morning, in the midst of the controversy, I was talking on the phone with a friend of mine who is the program director for a sports station in the Midwest. He knew I opposed gay marriage, and I knew he was for it. But I didn't think that was really the point here.

My friend said, "Come on, dude. I know what a big deal this is for you. But even you have to see how this is wrong. Answer me this: If Jesus owned a store, would he have said, 'We don't serve your kind' if gay people walked in the door?"

I tried to point out the obvious: "If Jesus owned a store, sure he would have sold groceries, because eating and shopping aren't sins. But he wouldn't have taken part in a gay wedding ceremony, because that would have been participating in a sinful relationship. The real question," I added, "is where does a gay person's right to marry end and my right to free exercise of my religion begin."

After about five seconds, he said, "Not following."

Doing the work that the American public school system clearly isn't doing itself, I explained: "If a state decides to pass a law—or more likely a court demands—that gay people can get married, fine; but if I have a constitutionally guaranteed right to the free exercise of my religion, I shouldn't be compelled to participate in something I think is sinful, like gay marriage. So if a gay couple gets turned down by a Christian photographer, they should find another freaking photographer!"

That's what life is supposed to be like in a free society—free to choose, freedom of association—but my friend, in this case, was just one example of the many in the sports media who took the Arizona law and twisted it into something it was absolutely not. Within hours of the story going national, *USA Today* ran headlines: "Arizona *Anti-Gay Bill* Is Shameful,"[1] "Arizona *Anti-Gay Bill*: Second Look,"[2] and, last but not least, "4 Things to Know about Arizona's *'Anti-Gay' Bill* [emphasis added in all headlines]."[3]

The sports media toed the same line. Pro Football Talk, which has become increasingly preachy, and less and less about pro football, ran headlines proclaiming, "MLB Issues Strong Statement regarding Proposed Arizona *Anti-Gay* Law"[4] and "Arizona Governor Vetoes *Anti-Gay Law*, Clearing Path for Super Bowl XLIX [emphasis added in both headlines]."[5] *Sporting News* joined in: "Super Bowl Could Nix Arizona If It Doesn't Back Off *Anti-Gay* Law [emphasis added]."[6]

The frenzy showcased activist journalism at its worst; they called it an "anti-gay bill" even though *nowhere* did the written legislation make reference to homosexuals, directly or indirectly. And in fact, if the Arizona legislature had wanted to allow businesses to refuse services to gays, it didn't have to do anything. As the *Christian Post* observed, "It is not currently illegal for a business to deny service to someone because they are gay. Some cities in Arizona have ordinances against it but there is no state law against it. If business owners in Arizona wanted to deny service to gays, they could do so in most of the state under current law."[7] Moreover, though the bill was definitely designed with Christians in mind, it wasn't exclusive to them. Muslims could have claimed RFRA protections from being forced to serve alcohol, and Hindus could have claimed protections from being forced to handle beef. Nor was the bill a return to "Jim Crow" segregation laws, as so many liberals claimed (conflating, as they almost always do, homosexuality with race). Paul Mirengoff, a lawyer writing at the popular blog *Power Line*, called such claims not only "false" but "hysterical."[8]

Which gets us down to the nitty-gritty. The purpose of this law was *not* to take rights away from gay people. Not a single gay person would have lost a single right as a result of the Arizona law. What the law ventured to do was to protect religious freedom—a freedom central to the founding of this country. If our public schools spent more time teaching American history and less time teaching how to put condoms on cucumbers, maybe more Americans, even in sports media, might have understood this.

So if the law wasn't anti-gay, which it clearly wasn't, and if it wasn't designed to usher in a new era of Jim Crow for gays, which it also clearly wasn't, then why all the controversy? Why did the NFL threaten to take away the Super Bowl if the law wasn't vetoed? Why did Major League Baseball condemn the law? Why did the sports media—all talk shows, websites, blogs, and TV shows included— spend the better part of a week attacking this bill like a hammerhead shark armed with mace and a stiletto? They attacked it, not because it was anti-gay, but because it was *pro*-Christian.

Sports media, as you might have noticed, have morphed into one of the largest and loudest forums for gay activism. No doubt about it. What's talked about much less, though, is how leftist producers and reporters have made sports media vociferously anti-Christian. The hysterical reaction of the sports world to a law limiting *government coercion* of religious people to perform what they consider immoral acts tells us all we need to know about where Christians stand with the liberal sports media. As Paul Mirengoff wrote on *Power Line*:

> *First*, it seems fundamentally wrong to deny someone service at, say, a restaurant or a gas station because of his or her sexual orientation (although doing so is not currently banned by Arizona state law). Likewise, it seems fundamentally wrong for a photographer to refuse to take, say, a passport photo of a person because of his or her sexual orientation. But *second*, it also seems fundamentally wrong to require a photographer who believes, based on sincere religious conviction, that gay marriage is immoral to participate in a gay marriage celebration by photographing it [emphasis in original].[9]

Precisely right, and this was a distinction that the photographers themselves made. They were perfectly happy to take portraits of gay people. What they objected to was participating in a ceremony they thought was immoral.

For most of us, America is about liberty, but no one in the mainstream media sports world seemed to acknowledge or care that there was anything wrong with forcing Christians to violate their religious beliefs. Gay rights trump Christian rights every time. Pro Football Talk took to Twitter to condemn the Arizona law: "We collectively wagged a finger at Russia for their anti-gay laws. Will we shrug at what Arizona may do? Hopefully the NFL won't."

Now, does Arizona remind you of Vladimir Putin's Russia? No? Me neither. But honestly I, too, have felt the need to wag a finger at former KGB colonel Vladimir Putin (I'll let you guess which one) for a number of reasons. But his stance on gay issues has never been one of them. Not that I'm okay with anybody being persecuted for anything, but if Pro Football Talk were to take a break from trying to be a gay *Pravda*, it might notice that there's more to Putin's Russia than anti-gay prejudice, like, you know, torture, court fixing, suppression of a free press, state-sanctioned murder, and even the invasion of Ukraine. But for sports media no international issues can compete with gay issues.

ESPN host Colin Cowherd basically didn't talk sports for an entire day so he could deal with the Arizona law. He even took to Twitter to challenge Christians directly: "For Christians saying 'a photographer has right to deny lesbian couple'. Do you deny couples who have had premarital sex too? Hmmm."

Hmmm, indeed. How many couples who have had premarital sex, in Cowherd's hypothetical example, would ask the photographers to join them in fornication or to photograph it? I think most people would agree that the photographers would have a right to say no. The gay couple in New Mexico was *explicitly demanding* that the photographers participate in an act that the photographers believed to be immoral. The real issue is not whether we're all sinners (the Christian answer to that is yes) but when it is legally acceptable to compel someone to violate his or her conscience. It's pretty amazing, isn't it, how gay-bandwagon sportscasters don't give a flip about freedom of conscience?

And if you really wanted to be serious about it, which you can't be in a tweet, a Christian can believe that fornication is a sin, but that a sin can be forgiven before a couple enters into a holy marriage, and that marriage is by nature and by God's design definable as a monogamous, heterosexual union. A homosexual marriage, by contrast, is, in a Christian view, a violation of natural law, contrary to God's design, and wrong—in other words, a sin. Is that so hard to understand? It's a view that, not so very long ago, was held nearly universally in this country and is now almost universally condemned by the progressive commissars who run sports media.

And think about it for a second: If you were gay, why would you seek out a Christian photographer to shoot your wedding? I mean, you've seen the kids who go to film and photography school; most of them look like malnourished, hipster baristas. There was certainly no shortage of photographers in New Mexico happy to photograph a gay commitment ceremony. Yet the gay couple in question deliberately chose a small photography business run by a Christian couple and then sued them when the photographers wouldn't violate their religious beliefs. Is that the American way?

I wouldn't want to force a Muslim photographer to come to my wedding and watch me pound Jäger shots and dance poorly to bad classic rock while manhandling my wife (I film that stuff myself anyway). And who would, exactly, want to hire someone morally opposed to their union to capture their special day? A person trying to make a political point, maybe? Or someone trying to rub someone else's nose in it? To many of us, that might seem ill-mannered, mean, or vindictive, but the sports media were more than willing to jump in and take their shots at the Christian photographers and the lawmakers who tried to defend freedom of religion.

Pardon the Interruption's Tony Kornheiser, for one, wasted no time in flushing public discourse down the proverbial crapper. He did more than demand the NFL move the Super Bowl if SB 1062 became law. In a flight of ridiculous hyperbole, he alleged that if it did become law, gay football player Michael Sam "could not buy a ticket possibly to the Super Bowl. Arizona has become in recent years the most recalcitrant, backward-looking state in the country when it comes to social change."[10] Kornheiser couldn't resist the reductio ad Hitlerum. Regarding gays in Arizona, he asked: "How are they supposed to be identified? Should they wear a yellow star? Because my people went through that at one point."[11]

The utter clownery of his statement probably deserves its own chapter, but in the interest of time (and my sanity) I'll confine it to a few lines. First of all, under what circumstances would Michael Sam not be allowed to buy a ticket to the Super Bowl? This is the difference between a journalist and an ideologue. If Kornheiser had approached the subject as a journalist, he would have acknowledged that the bill did not prevent Michael Sam, or any gay person, from going to the Super Bowl or any other public venue. But he wasn't approaching it as a journalist; he was approaching it as a gay-rights activist, which is why he invoked not only the image of Jim Crow–like exclusion but also the Nazis.

The motivation behind the bill was to defend the First Amendment, hardly a calling card of National Socialism. Breitbart.com sports editor Daniel Flynn noted the law's clear intent was to allow "citizens to invoke their free exercise of religion as a legal protection against prosecution."[12] It said nothing about homosexuals at all, let alone marking them for identification. And if Kornheiser really wanted to play the Nazi game, he might have acknowledged, if he had any knowledge at all, that Catholic priests, readily identifiable by their collars, had their own wing at the Buchenwald death camps, having been sent there by the Nazis for opposing a pagan regime. No one was talking about coercing gays with this Arizona law; the lawmakers were trying to *prevent* the coercion of Christians. So who is playing Nazi here—the lawmakers who want to defend religious freedom or the sports media bozos who want to expunge Christians' (and Jews' and Muslims' and others') First Amendment rights?

And that brings us to another point—and a bigger one. There's something far darker and more sinister going on here than simple media overreaction. Likening Christians to Nazis, which Kornheiser did without using the word *Christian*, has become a sort of media trope. Right after the NFL draft in April 2010, Boston-based sports radio host Fred Toettcher searched for words to describe the scene of white Christian athlete Tim Tebow's draft party at his parent's home, and boy did Toettcher paint a picture: "It looked like some kind of Nazi rally.... So lily-white is what I'm trying to say. Yeah, Stepford Wives."[13]

Hmm, interesting use of words there. Question, though: Do you think that Tim Tebow's draft party was the first "lily-white" draft party that Fred Toettcher had ever seen? After all, Toettcher has been a media guy for years, and he's probably been watching the draft his whole life. He's undoubtedly seen dozens of other white athletes surrounded by their "Stepford Wives" and their families.

Yet Toettcher never used the term "Nazi rally" to describe any of their draft parties. Why? Because when Toettcher was watching the scene of Tebow's family at his draft party, he wasn't looking at them as people, *he was looking at what they stand for.* And in Toettcher's mind, what they stand for, coupled with their "lily-white" surroundings, equals hate. Because that's how he and many other prominent members of the sports media see Christians: Christianity equals intolerance, which equals hate, which equals racism, which equals bigotry. This despite the fact that the Tebows have probably done more for nonwhite people in one weekend of charitable works than Fred Toettcher, Tony Kornheiser, and any other lefty sportscaster you want to throw in there have done in the last ten years.

Of course, many sportscasters are subtler than that, but with a similar agenda: they don't like Christianity, or at the very least they want Christians to be silent. For instance, in October 2013, a group of Seattle Seahawks, four players and two coaches, released a video entitled *The Making of a Champion: Seattle Seahawks*. Led by long snapper Clint Gresham and including quarterback Russell Wilson, they talked about their love of the game; how being a champion means not just winning at football, but at life; and why they play the game for a higher purpose, to honor and glorify God. Inspiring, right? Harmless, right? A perfect antidote to so much NFL news overlapping with the crime pages, right? Wrong. At least according to Pro Football Talk's Mike Florio, who, after watching the video, wrote: "The not-so-subtle message from *The Making of a Champion: Seattle Seahawks* is that Christian believers always thrive, and that the Seahawks are a team of Christian believers. While we respect everyone's right to believe whatever they choose to believe (and I'm a lifelong Roman Catholic), there's a line that easily can be crossed when employment and religion become intertwined."[14]

This is such a magical pile of crap. No one ever remotely suggested, either in the fifteen-minute film or outside of it, that Christian belief is *a condition* of being a Seattle Seahawk. The video was not produced by the Seahawks organization; it was put together by a handful of coaches and players who happen to work and play for the Seahawks and who specifically emphasize that they found faith while looking *beyond* their football glory. It is never stated or even implied that the Seahawks are "a team of Christian believers." Florio seems to take the position that it's fine to be a Christian in sports as long as you never talk about it. I wonder how many other groups he would apply that to. It seems like we talked about nothing else in the sports world for weeks but about how great it was that football player Michael Sam is gay—and I'm sure a fifteen-minute film about him would be hailed for its "courage" and replayed endlessly on ESPN. But a short, innocuous film about how Christian faith has inspired these players and coaches to become better people? Nah, that's too much. Florio gets it wrong too when he says that the "not-so-subtle message" of the film "is that Christian believers always thrive." Really? One of the coaches interviewed cites the courage shown by a Christian player after a *career-ending* knee injury as one of the things that attracted him to the faith. One of the main points of the movie is not that faith will reward you with worldly success but that faith can help you overcome adversity, that it can fill the void you might feel *even after you have worldly success*. Florio, as is so common with sports reporters writing about religion, prefers to deal in negative stereotypes and clichés rather than reality. You also might think that as a lawyer he would have a better grasp of the First Amendment and the right of Christian players and coaches to talk about their Christian beliefs without scare-mongering about religious tests that don't exist.

Sometimes sportscasters take a different tack, simply ignoring expressions of Christianity and replacing them with their own obsessions. In August 2012, Gabby Douglas wrapped up an incredible performance at the London Olympic Games, becoming the first black female to win the gold in the women's gymnastics all-around competition. In an NBC interview, Douglas said, "It is everything I thought it would be; being the Olympic champion, it definitely is an amazing feeling. And I give all the glory to God. It's kind of a win-win situation. The glory goes up to Him and the blessings fall down on me."[15]

Her Twitter account has stated that she loves "my family, dogs & most importantly God :),"[16] and as the *Christian Post* reported, she tweeted after her Olympic triumph: "Let all that I am praise the LORD; may I never forget the good things he does for me."[17]

But NBC Sports places God in a different place of priority, and that place is nowhere. Completely ignoring what Douglas had said about what her victory meant to her, and the message she wanted people to take from it (which we in the sports media used to call…you know…the story), Bob Costas determined to make sure this Jesus guy got no play, and let us know what the media thought the real story was: "There are some young African American girls out there who tonight are saying to themselves, hey, I'd like to try that too."[18]

Wow, just wow. One of the worst aspects of today's race-obsessed, gay-obsessed media is that we can't even enjoy a moment like Gabby Douglas's thrilling victory in London without having the obligatory PC bull thrown in there by somebody like Costas. Who gave a rip that night that Gabby Douglas was black? Answer? Outside of the NBC Sports studios? Close to zero. For all the talk about how race shouldn't matter, the liberal media sure are quick to bring it up, aren't they?

Point being, *any* little girl could have and should have been inspired by Gabby Douglas that night, white or black. While many were angry (justifiably) on Twitter with Costas for needlessly bringing race into the discussion, people missed the bigger story: It wasn't just that Costas had needlessly "gone there" as far as race. It was that he went there so he could squelch the message of an athlete who was obviously motivated by a higher power. Bob Costas treated Gabby Douglas the same way the sports media treated Tony Dungy after Super Bowl XLI. Though the Colts head coach repeatedly and strenuously claimed that his victory was all about God, the sports media did everything in their power to make sure that the story had nothing to do with God and everything to do with race, with Dungy being the first black head coach to win a Super Bowl. Costas could have said that girls across America could use Gabby Douglas's kind of faith to overcome obstacles, or he could have just gone to a commercial, but by injecting the sports media's petty, tired political agenda into a story that had absolutely nothing to do with it, Costas robbed Gabby Douglas of her moment and what it meant to *her* (and her fellow Christians)—something he would not have dared do if she had been gay or Muslim.

To say that the liberal sports media have a blind spot when it comes to religion is to grotesquely understate the problem. In December 2013, ESPN informed the Cardinal Glennon Children's Foundation that they would refuse to air the foundation's commercial during the Christmas season. The commercial encouraged viewers to send get-well wishes to kids with cancer and messages of support to their moms and dads.

So why did ESPN refuse to run the ad? Because, according to Dan Buck, the executive director of the Cardinal Glennon Children's Foundation, ESPN thought the words "Jesus" and "God" in the foundation's Christmas message were "problematic."[19]

"Jesus" and "God" are "problematic" for ESPN? In a *Christmas* commercial? In a Christmas commercial asking for messages of hope to seriously sick kids? Eventually, the worldwide leader in sports came around and aired the commercial, but only after Bill O'Reilly slammed the network on his Fox News television show, *The O'Reilly Factor*.

What's even richer about all this is that ESPN cited their advocacy standards, which prevent them from airing political or religious commercials, as a defense for not airing the Cardinal Glennon commercial. This is the same network, you'll recall, that allowed its employees to tweet their support of Trayvon; the same network with a show hosted by outspoken leftist Keith Olbermann; the same network that made a seventh-round NFL draft pick its lead story on a Sunday morning over the results of an NBA playoff game solely because the draftee was gay, and made sure we got to see him at length snogging his boyfriend; the same network whose talking heads bashed the state of Arizona because its legislature tried to protect freedom of religion.

Not just ESPN but sports media in general have no problem jumping into the fray on political issues, even when they have absolutely nothing to do with sports. In the fall of 2013, Craig James was fired from his job at Fox Sports as a college football analyst only one week into his time there. So you're thinking to yourself: *Wow. Craig James was at ESPN for years and only lasted one week at Fox Sports. What could he have said in only one week to get himself fired?* The answer to that would be *nothing*. Because Craig James wasn't fired over anything he said at Fox Sports; he was fired over religious views he expressed while running to replace Kay Bailey Hutchison as the next U.S. senator from Texas. As reported by the American Family Association: "As a candidate during a Texas U.S. Senate campaign in 2010, Craig James said his Christian faith clearly outlined his position on gay marriage and pledged he would not support same-sex unions. He also stated he was 'adamantly opposed to abortion.'"[20]

Now, again, this wasn't something that happened during a college football broadcast, where, between breaking down the zone read and the trips-right formation, all of a sudden James decided to make a comment on gay marriage or abortion. This happened on the campaign trail, while he was running for a Senate seat. So, essentially, Fox Sports fired Craig James for the thoughts in his head, thoughts that happen to be shared by tens of millions of Christian, pro-life, pro–traditional marriage Americans—but by hardly anyone in sports media. Craig James filmed one episode of a regional college football show for Fox, a show that came off completely without incident, and was then fired.

What happened next was high comedy. The *Dallas Morning News* reported that the decision to fire James came from Fox Sports management's becoming aware that James had expressed opposition to gay marriage, quoting a source as saying, "We just asked ourselves how Craig's statements would play in our human resources department. He couldn't say those things here."[21] A senior vice president from Fox even told media outlets that James had been terminated because of his views on same-sex marriage. James told Breitbart.com: "I was shocked that my personal religious beliefs were not only the reason for Fox Sports firing me but I was completely floored when I read stories quoting Fox Sports representatives essentially saying that people of faith are banned from working at Fox Sports. That is not right and surely someone made a terrible mistake."[22]

The "mistake" might have had legal complications because firing James for his religious beliefs sounds like a civil rights violation, doesn't it? According to court documents that were obtained by Breitbart.com: "Fox Sports President Eric Shanks admitted in a deposition that a senior VP at Fox Sports told media outlets that sportscaster Craig James was fired from the network because of his support for traditional marriage. Shanks says that statement to the press was untrue."[23]

Which is kind of funny, because if James wasn't fired over his stance on same-sex marriage, then why was he fired? Was he fired over one recording of a regional college football show where, according to all concerned, everything went fine? At the time of this writing, the matter is still being fought out in the courts. But anyone can see what's going on here. Whoever hired Craig James at Fox Sports forgot that the sports media aren't really the sports media anymore. They are simply another branch of the anti-Christian gay-rights movement, and by the time somebody realized this mistake, it was too late. The best part of this, though, is Fox Sports' alleged justification for firing James, worth repeating: "We just asked ourselves how Craig's statements would play in our human resources department. He couldn't say those things here."[24]

Really? James told Breitbart.com: "I have worked in broadcasting for twenty-four years and have always treated my colleagues with respect and dignity regardless of their background or personal beliefs. I believe it is essential in our business to maintain professional relationships with people from a diverse background and have tolerance for those of different beliefs. I have never discussed my faith while broadcasting and it has never been an issue until now."[25]

I seriously doubt that Craig James, who survived for years at ESPN, a network at least as if not more liberal than Fox Sports, would have been walking around HR, or the watercooler, spouting his beliefs on gay marriage. One does not survive long in the sports media by doing such things; James's views on these issues didn't become public until *after* he left ESPN and *before* he got to Fox Sports. There's a reason for that.

But here's the kicker: while Fox apparently had problems with James's privately held religious beliefs on gay marriage, they apparently had no worries at all about the anti-Christian and racist commentary of one of their leading columnists, Jason Whitlock. After Jeremy Lin lit up the Lakers for thirty-eight points, Whitlock tweeted: "Some lucky lady in NYC is gonna feel a couple inches of pain tonight."[26] That line is as crass as it is racist. But Asian American penis jokes, especially if they're made at the expense of an openly *Christian* Asian American, must go down just fine at Fox Sports' HR Department. Fox Sports' most recognizable columnist can go on Twitter, *while employed by Fox and while representing them*, and show the mental maturity of a filthy-minded, racist thirteen-year-old baiting the Asian Christian kid for his beliefs about chastity; meanwhile, Craig James, *while not on the clock*, can't speak about his religious convictions in a political campaign? Really, Fox Sports, those are your standards?

But Fox Sports isn't alone in its hypocrisy. Keith Olbermann left ESPN to talk politics at MSNBC, and while doing so racked up one of the longest and most distinguished lists of quotable absurdity you're ever going to hear. In January 2010, Olbermann likened the American healthcare system to terrorism and accused the Bush administration of signing off on the deaths of thousands of Americans:

> What would you do, sir, if terrorists were killing 45,000 people every year in this country? Well, the current health care system, the insurance companies, and those who support them are doing just that.... Because they die individually of disease and not disaster, [radio host] Neal Boortz and those who ape him in office and out, approve their deaths, all 45,000 of them—a year—in America. Remind me again, who are the terrorists?[27]

In 2010, he blamed Rush Limbaugh for the Oklahoma City bombing:

> "What was the more likely cause of the Oklahoma City bombing: talk radio or Bill Clinton and Janet Reno's hands-on management of Waco, the Branch Davidian compound?..." Obviously, the answer is talk radio. Specifically Rush Limbaugh's hate radio.... Frankly, Rush,

you have that blood on your hands now and you have had it for 15 years.[28]

And in 2006, Olbermann opined that the U.S. government, under President George W. Bush, was a bigger threat to Americans than terrorists:

> We now face what our ancestors faced at other times of exaggerated crisis and melodramatic fear-mongering: A government more dangerous to our liberty than is the enemy it claims to protect us from.... We have not before codified the poisoning of habeas corpus, that wellspring of protection from which all essential liberties flow. You, sir, have now befouled that spring. You, sir, have now given us chaos and called it order. You, sir, have now imposed sub-jugation and called it freedom.... These things you have done, Mr. Bush—they would be the beginning of the end of America.[29]

And yet, despite this plethora of crazed commentary, Keith Olbermann was *re*-hired by ESPN in August 2013. If Olbermann were the only one at the "Worldwide Leader" playing the fool, we might have cause for hope, but unfortunately his number is legion at ESPN.

In the summer of 2012, Nebraska football assistant coach Ron Brown spoke out against a gay and transgender anti-discrimination law then under consideration in Omaha. Brown, using his constitu-tional right (and, dare I say, God-given right), spoke out against the law based on his Christian beliefs. According to ESPN.com, "Brown challenged ordinance sponsor Ben Gray and other [city council] mem-bers to remember the Bible does not condone homosexuality. He told council members they would be held to 'great accountability for the decision you are making.'"[30]

The University of Nebraska recognized Brown's right to speak out on the issue, but that did not fly for ESPN's Gene Wojciechowski, who, apparently forgetting what country he's in, called for coach Ron Brown's firing "if he continues to confuse faith with a person's fundamental right not to be discriminated against."[31]

Paul Wilson, writing for Fox News, showed that not all the media are insane and asked the pertinent question: "What exactly is the 'fundamental right not to be discriminated against,' anyway?" At least for the sports media, "Politically-correct rights concocted by sports journalists apparently trump arcane rights such as freedom of speech or religion."[32] Funny, too, how this "fundamental right" of nondiscrimination never seems to apply when idiot sports writers want to attack Christians for exercising their right to free speech.

In fact, ESPN actively discriminates against Christians, even when they are engaged in nonpartisan civic activities. ESPN had no problem airing Rock the Vote ads to encourage young people to vote, even plugging on its X Games site the participation of skateboard "legend" Tony Hawk. But it nixed an ad featuring NASCAR driver Blake Koch for a nonpartisan voting group called Rise Up and Register because the Rise Up and Register website linked to Koch's website, which linked to . . . wait for it . . . Christian ministries, and specifically to the "Be My Vote" campaign geared toward pro-lifers. Therefore, ESPN decided they could not air the ad. You get all that? A nonpartisan voter registration ad that linked, not directly, but to a second- and even third-party Christian ministry and pro-life group was enough to get the ad nixed because it compromised the network's political and religious advocacy standards. But Rock the Vote, whose celebrity endorsers lean heavily left while the organization itself is professedly nonpartisan, was not problematic at all. I think we all know why.

As if there weren't already enough to loathe and despise about the self-righteous, anti-Christian bigots who masquerade as our sports media today, their smugness over their assumed sense of wit and intelligence on matters they know nothing about is the icing on the cake. In December 2012, Tigers outfielder Torii Hunter was asked how he would feel about having a gay player on his team, and was quoted as saying: "For me, as a Christian…I will be uncomfortable because in all my teachings and all my learning, biblically, it's not right. It will be difficult and uncomfortable."[33]

Hunter came out later and said those quotations were taken out of context and misrepresented what he actually said. Unfortunately, that's beside the point. After hearing those quotations from Hunter, CBS Sports' Dayn Perry decided to surf the Google in an attempt to sound far smarter than he actually is: "Hunter is of course entitled to his personal beliefs" (which is always what liberals say, just before they take a giant dump on your personal beliefs), "although one wonders whether he is similarly affronted by, say, shellfish and neatly maintained beards, which are also forbidden by the holiness code of Leviticus."[34]

This did not escape the attention of the Media Research Center's Matt Philbin, who executed a clean takedown of Perry: "Great argument. Here's the problem: The New Testament lifts dietary restrictions, just as it no longer requires the sacrifices demanded in Leviticus. But the New Testament explicitly reaffirms Leviticus' injunction on homosexuality (I Corinthians 6:9–10 and Romans 1:26)."[35]

Stay in your lane, Perry.

But Dayn Perry isn't the only one who has tried to have some fun with ol' Leviticus. Boxer Manny Pacquiao, who is a Catholic and a politician in his home country of the Philippines, came out against gay marriage, as you might expect from a Catholic in an overwhelmingly Catholic country. The media, however, decided that what really happened here was that Pacquiao had come out in favor of gay executions. In an article, Granville Ampong of the Examiner.com chronicled and contrasted Pacquiao's views on same-sex marriage with those of President Obama's. Pacquiao had drawn strong distinctions between himself and President Obama: "God's words first...obey God's law first before considering the laws of man...."[36]

Sigh. President Pacquiao has such a nice ring to it. Vladimir Putin would definitely think twice before crossing that guy. But anyhow, Pacquiao's quotation wasn't what provoked the wrath of the liberal sports media. About two paragraphs down from Pacquiao's actual words, the writer, Ampong, threw in this passage from Leviticus: "If a man lies with a man as one lies with a woman, both of them have done what is detestable. They must be put to death; their blood will be on their own heads."[37]

Now, the article clearly doesn't quote Pacquiao as having actually said this; it merely includes the quotation to give some frame of reference (though outdated) for biblical teachings on homosexuality. But that little factoid did nothing to stop the anti-Christian media from unleashing the Kraken of Crazy. Almost immediately, the left-wing group *ThinkProgress* tweeted out a message demanding that Nike cut off Pacquiao from their client list: "Dear @Nike: Are you going to continue to sponsor boxer Manny Pacquiao, who is engaging in hate speech against gays?"[38]

The liberal Courage Campaign jumped into the fray as well: "Homophobia+Violence= @Nike? Join us in telling Nike to drop #homophobic boxer #MannyPacquiao http://bit.ly/IWUinB #DropManny."[39]

But again, Pacquiao never said the quotation. After the dustup, Pacquiao explained: "I didn't say that, that's a lie.... I didn't know that quote from Leviticus because I haven't read the Book of Leviticus yet."[40] And before anyone jumps on Pacquiao (as if they'd dare) for not knowing what he's talking about, it's important to remember that Christianity isn't about memorizing the Bible. It's a statement of historical facts and moral teaching. Pacquiao knows the Catholic Church teaches the sinfulness of homosexual behavior. He's right about that, even if he couldn't quote you Leviticus or the passages from Corinthians or Romans—and as you probably know, the Catholic Church doesn't endorse a death penalty for homosexuals; the Church's current pope has even washed the feet of AIDS victims, exemplifying Christ's teachings on charity and service. I wonder how many sports journalists could say the same.

The author of the article that sparked the brouhaha, Granville Ampong, weighed in to clarify what he had written:

> Nowhere in my supposition and integration of my interview with Pacquiao did I mention that Pacquiao recited this Leviticus 20:13 nor did I imply that Pacquiao had quoted such. I have simply reminded in my column how God made it clear in the Old Testament time that such practice of same-sex marriage is detestable and strictly forbidden, in as much as God wants to encourage [in] his people practices that lead to health and happiness and fullness of life.[41]

Now follow me on a journey to an imaginary place where the media aren't on an anti-Christian crusade to make the world safe for gay marriage. In that wonderful, but completely pretend, paradise, having the author of the article explicitly confirm that Pacquiao never quoted Leviticus would put an end to the story and might even lead to a few media apologies. Instead, in reality, all it did was enrage the media further. Days after Pacquiao denied quoting Leviticus and Ampong confirmed his denial, *ThinkProgress* took to Twitter and showed that they neither think nor have they progressed: "UPDATE: Did Pacquiao cite the Leviticus 'put to death' verse or not? A new statement suggests he did: http://bit.ly/Kt5gGB."[42]

The Courage Campaign tweeted: "Stand with millions of LGBT and fair minded-people the world over. Drop Manny Pacquiao now. Hatred surely does not = Nike."[43]

ESPN's *Grantland* website went even further, offering use of their site to Laurel Fantauzzo, a well-known lesbian activist, so she could display her contempt for Pacquiao and the Catholic Church—and mind you, this was a day *after* Pacquiao denied having quoted Leviticus. Here are just a few pearls from Fantauzzo's screed:

> I know, though, that you [Pacquiao] also don't want me to be married. I know you think this is a perfectly reasonable, justified stand to take against me. You're like a lot of Filipinos: Catholic. Powerfully, post-colonially Catholic....
>
> I've stood in front of the Black Nazarene in Quiapo Church that you pray to after each fight.... I've felt the power and the grace of it. I get it.... When you grow up Filipina—or Italiapina, as I did—your parents give you Catholicism as a kind of heavy gift. A centuries-old guide for every life transition a human can go through. Birth, death, the burden of any wrongdoing, and, yes, marriage. But as I grew older and realized the dreaded word applied to me—lesbian—I realized the Church was what I'd have

to feint and duck; the Church's cruel, untrue dictates about me were what I'd have to dance with and defeat....

When I faced Proposition 22, Proposition 8, DOMA, Amendment 1, and too many dictates from the Church, and relatives, and leaders like you, who called me disordered, dangerous, diseased, doomed, how did I survive?...[44]

As you can probably tell, this isn't just some random, concerned lesbian woman whom *Grantland* selected for this article; this is a renowned leftist, anti-Catholic activist. As Matthew Balan wrote at NewsBusters.org:

The website's [*Grantland*] editor noted in their short bio of Fantauzzo that she was a "2011 Fulbright Scholar to the Philippines. She's currently an Arts Fellow at the University of Iowa Master of Fine Arts in Nonfiction program." Shamelessly, the unnamed editor added, "Ladies, she's also currently single." But, Grantland completely left out the radical activism in her background.

Astraea Lesbian Foundation for Justice gave a $10,000 grant to the writer in 2009–2010, and disclosed that she "has contributed to AfterEllen and Go Magazine, among other publications. She also founded the popular We Are Not the Enemy photo blog in response to California's Proposition 8." In September 2011, she wrote an article for the online magazine The FilAm ("a magazine for Filipino Americans in New York"), where she promoted the so-called RH ("reproductive health") bill in the Philippines, which would legalize abortifacients and contraceptives, and is staunchly opposed by the Catholic bishops in the country.[45]

In other words, the truth of the story didn't matter. The fact that Manny Pacquiao never said what he was accused of saying didn't matter. His opposition to President Obama, and references to God and God's laws, were enough for the media to trample all over journalistic principle. The only truth that ESPN's *Grantland* and others aired was Laurel Fantauzzo's "truth," because they feel exactly the same way she does. They believe in blanket gay marriage, they see the Catholic Church as bigoted and oppressive, and they agree with her so much that they don't care if they have to lie, cover up, or fabricate quotations in order to go against the Church.

The anti-Christian bias of the American sports establishment is reflected in international sports bodies as well. In 2009, FIFA, the organizing body that administrates international professional soccer, disciplined a couple of Brazilian superstar players for overt displays of Christianity during a match.

According to the *Daily Mail*:

> Stars including £56 million Real Madrid forward Kaka and captain Lucio revealed T-shirts with devout slogans such as "I Belong to Jesus" and "I Love God" during the Confederations Cup final last month.
>
> Now FIFA has risked accusations of being "anti-religious" by reminding Brazil of its guidelines banning players from making displays of a personal, religious or political nature on the football pitch.[46]

FIFA seemed to express no concern at all, though, when labeled anti-religious. In fact, international soccer regulators felt so unconcerned that they immediately took FIFA's ball and ran with it. The head of soccer in Denmark went even further than FIFA, calling for an immediate ban on any and all religious statements. He said, "Just as we reject political manifestations, we should also say no to religious ones. There are too many risks involved in clubs, for example, with people of different religious faiths."[47]

According to the *Daily Mail*, the specific rule in question that the pesky Brazilian Christians violated, called Law 4, reads: "Players must not reveal undergarments showing slogans or advertising. The basic compulsory equipment must not have any political, religious or personal statements."[48]

FIFA, however, turned a 180 when the religious concerns of Muslims came into question. In 2011, the Iranian women's national team withdrew from a game against Jordan because they weren't allowed to wear their traditional Muslim headscarves.[49] Now mind you, this was not a religious "undergarment" of the kind that got the Christian Brazilian players punished. This was a loud, proud, in-your-face outer garment, worn on the head, which would be seen by all.

So what did FIFA do? Did they tell the Iranian women's national team that since FIFA had already banned undergarments with Christian statements, it would be completely and totally hypocritical for them to turn around and allow Muslims to wear outer garments that serve as religious symbols? I'll save you the suspense: they did not.

Instead, FIFA, which had previously regarded headgear as unsafe, reversed course. The BBC described what happened next:

> Following a request from the Asian Football Confederation, the IFAB (International Football Association Board) allowed for their safety to be tested during the trial.
>
> At the annual general meeting at FIFA's headquarters, IFAB members also voted to introduce a new law that will punish players who display messages on T-shirts underneath their club's kit.

The rule change, which will come into effect from 1 June, amends Law 4 of the game, which relates to players' equipment.[50]

So not only did the governing body *not* vote to reaffirm the ban on religious headgear, but they voted to make *another law* to prevent players from wearing religiously themed undergarments—just in case Christian players tried to bring back their Jesus shirts.

The obvious message: religious symbolism really isn't all that bad, just so long as it's not Christian religious symbolism. If it's Muslim symbolism, they'll "safety" test it and then change the rules in your favor. FIFA clearly isn't worried about being called anti-religious or anti-Christian. They just don't want to be called anti-Muslim.

Similarly, the sports media aren't at all worried about mocking the sexual ethics of Christians, because they regard these ethics as ridiculous and repressive.

Still, you might have thought that someone like Lolo Jones, a Christian and quite possibly the only person in the entire London Olympic Village not utilizing her share of the more than 150,000 prophylactics provided to the athletes, would at least get some begrudging media praise for her willpower alone.

And you would be wrong. During the run up to her 2012 appearance in the London Games, Jones gained a lot of attention for her stated desire to abstain from sex until marriage. The *New York Times*, which abstains from nothing except objective, fact-based reporting, published a piece lashing out at Jones, saying she "received far greater publicity than any other American track and field athlete competing in the London Games. This was based not on achievement but on her exotic beauty and on a sad and cynical marketing campaign."[51]

Uh-huh. Yet the *New York Times* had no problem adding to the publicity of Michael Sam, who gained enormous media attention not because of his achievements on the football field but because of his homosexuality. Michael Sam wasn't even the best player on his own defense at Missouri, but the *Times* confidently asserted in February 2014 that, "Mr. Sam, 24, is projected to be chosen in the early rounds of the N.F.L. draft in May, ordinarily a path to a prosperous pro career."[52]

The statement was laughable to anyone who actually watches college football. Sam was, at best, a mid-round pick, and more likely not draft worthy at all, but he was a symbol of a cause the *Times* is at pains to hype—and that cause is not chastity, or heterosexuality.

Rookie Michael Sam was released before the start of the 2014 NFL season by the St. Louis Rams, the team that drafted him. But that wasn't the end of the story. ESPN's Stephen A. Smith spilled the beans on the league's behind-the-scenes efforts to make sure Sam landed on an NFL roster:

> According to sources I have in the NFL, the league did call a few teams. They did want teams to take Michael Sam *because obviously we see what kind of movement they're gearing for* [emphasis added], and what their support of Michael Sam, who we all know, came out, acknowledged that he was gay before the draft and ultimately this is something that Roger Goodell and the NFL support and they want their teams to support. But other teams weren't too receptive to taking him on once the St. Louis Rams cut him.
>
> So in steps Jerry Jones [owner of the Dallas Cowboys], coming to the aid of the NFL and making a splash with his

willingness to bring this guy on board to the practice squad.[53]

The "movement" the league was gearing for was a liberal, sports media freak-out of epic proportions had Sam not made an NFL roster. Which is what prompted the NFL's cowardly eleventh-hour scramble to ensure (with who knows what kind of promises and assurances attached) that somebody signed Sam to a team. As *Sports Illustrated*'s Peter King said, "Now Sam and the NFL avoided a nightmare situation when he signed with the practice squad of the Dallas Cowboys."[54] Though the Cowboys spared the NFL a public-relations nightmare, they eventually, and quietly, released Michael Sam as well.

So let's take stock of where the sports media's values really lie. Lolo Jones refuses to have sex before marriage, because she's a Christian. But because she refuses to allow herself to become the carnal conquest of the Swedish curling team, her credibility as a star (despite her multiple indoor track championships and ability to qualify for the Olympics in two different sports) is disparaged; her personal story is nothing but a "sad and cynical marketing campaign."

Yet Michael Sam's personal story became so incredibly vital to the liberal sports media that not only did they vastly overinflate his pre-draft status, but they succeeded in threatening the NFL with a PR disaster unless he made, even temporarily and on a practice squad, some team's regular season roster.

Yeah, there's nothing sad or cynical about that.

The depth of contempt and outright hatred the sports media hold for Christianity probably deserves its own book, not just its own chapter. The American sports media are a loud and proud focal point in the gay-activist movement, and they've branded Christianity as the premier roadblock between where they are and where they're trying to go. Most of us see Christianity as a saving, nurturing grace in our lives, whereas the sports media see it as an obstacle, something to be overcome and ultimately left behind in the dust. You can agree with where they stand or disagree with it, but the fact is that it's not the sports media's job to disparage Christianity. They can leave that to others. How about just reporting on sports—they have a tough enough time doing that.

CHAPTER THREE

KNAVES ON THE WARPATH

There's a unique feeling-out process that happens when you get to a new radio station. Of course, there's one at any new job, but in radio, where the business is driven by opinions and passionate takes instead of sales or closing the big account, the process tends to be more about one's worldview. So, not surprisingly, I did not have to wait very long for the first ideological probe to be administered when I started at my second sports station. It happened innocently enough, hanging out in the studio's break room with a bunch of producers and fellow hosts. Joking, laughing, and messing around on the internet, all of a sudden the topic turned to the Redskins' name change. Since I was the new guy, and since I was from Washington, D.C., I knew that in only a matter of seconds the inevitable question would be thrown my way:

PRODUCER: So, man, what do you think about the Redskins' name? Do you think they should change it?

ME: What do you mean? Why should they change it?

PRODUCER: You know, because it's so offensive to Native
Americans!

ME: No. I think when the state of Oklahoma changes its
name, that's when the Redskins should change their name.

This response earned me some quizzical looks. So I elaborated.

ME: Oklahoma literally translates to "Red People" in the
Choctaw language. How is that any better than, or any
different from, Redskin? Indiana translates into "land of
the Indians," and Indianapolis translates into "City in the
land of the Indians." Are you going to force every city and
state that alludes to "red people" or "Indians" to change
its name after you're done forcing the Redskins to change
theirs? Where does it end?

It didn't take long to realize I had given the wrong answer; the
lively conversation faded to dead silence, and everyone became suddenly laser-focused on their computer screens, no longer interested in
discussing the Redskins and their "offensive" name, or anything else
for that matter. And so it goes. You see, contrary to the idea that a
sports newsroom or other media outlet should be a bastion of free-
thinking and communication that would welcome dissenting points
of view, in reality they are a bastion of liberal group-think. "Questions" like the one my producers asked me are intended not just to
find out what you think but also to expose those beyond the pale of
liberal conventional wisdom.

That conventional wisdom includes the belief that changing the name of the Washington Redskins is now one of the leading civil rights issues of our time. In early 2012, during a *Sunday Night Football* halftime, Bob Costas referred to the team name as "a slur,"[1] which is laughable on several levels, including the fact that Costas and his fellow journalists have used the word countless times over decades of broadcasting and only recently discovered its alleged offensiveness. And answer me this: How many teams name themselves after a slur?

You might think that the liberal offensive to demand a name change, reaching all the way from the sports media to President Barack Obama, must be linked to some major public uproar. And you would be wrong.

In fact, according to an AP-Gfk poll conducted in April 2013, 79 percent of Americans *did not* think the Redskins should change their name; only 11 percent thought they should. *But, Dylan,* you might say, *who cares what "ordinary" Americans think about the Redskins' name? The important thing is what "Native Americans" think about it. If you ask them, I'll bet you get a different answer!*

And you'd be right. Indians gave a *much* different answer: According to a poll of 768 Native Americans taken by the University of Pennsylvania's National Annenberg Election Survey, when asked what they thought of the team name "Redskins," *90 percent* of Native American respondents said that they found the term "Redskin" *not offensive*. Only 9 percent thought it was offensive. It is not American Indians who are leading the charge to change team names; it is American liberals, *even against the wishes of American Indians*. In 2012, the state of North Dakota capitulated to pressure from the NCAA and dropped the "Fighting Sioux" as the nickname for the University of North Dakota's sports teams, *even though the Sioux of*

North Dakota's Spirit Lake Indian Reservation had voted in favor of keeping the nickname in 2010. As even ESPN.com felt obliged to acknowledge, reproducing an Associated Press report:

> Many American Indians lobbied for the name and logo to be kept, arguing that they reflected a positive image for their tribes. Eunice Davidson, an enrolled member of the Spirit Lake tribe and member of the committee to save the nickname, was too devastated to talk about the result, her husband Dave Davidson said.
>
> "I will be honest with you. I'm heartbroken and I'm ashamed of this state," Dave Davidson said. "On the other hand, there are a lot of wonderful people we have met in the course of this."
>
> Later, Eunice Davidson remarked that if she could speak to Dan Snyder, owner of the Washington Redskins, she would tell him, "I stand with him. I don't want our history to be forgotten."[2]

Funny, but you don't often hear voices like Eunice Davidson's on sports media, not because they don't exist—they're actually the majority—but because they don't fit the liberal sports media's narrative. If the sports networks went beyond the professional grievance-mongers, they might get somebody like Tommy Yazzie, superintendent of the Red Mesa School District for the Navajo Nation, who thinks tribes have more-important things to worry about than the name of the Washington Redskins:

> We just don't think that it [the Redskins' name] is an issue. There are more important things like busing our kids to

school, the water settlement, the land quality, the air that surrounds us. Those are issues we can take sides on. Society, they think it's more derogatory because of the recent discussions. In its pure form, a lot of Native American men, you go into the sweat lodge with what you've got— your skin. I don't see it as derogatory.[3]

Coincidentally, the nickname for the sports teams in the Red Mesa School District? The Redskins.

Why don't the sports networks give airtime to mainstream American Indian opinion on this issue? Maybe because they fear they would come across somebody like Robert Green, the longtime and recently retired chief of the Fredericksburg, Virginia, Patawomeck tribe, who said, among other things:

Frankly, the members of my tribe—the vast majority— don't find it offensive. I've been a Redskins fan for years. And to be honest with you, I would be offended if they did change it [the name, Redskins.... This is] an attempt by somebody...to completely remove the Indian identity from anything and pretty soon...you have a wipeout in society of any reference to Indian people.... You can't rewrite history—yes there were some awful, bad things done to our people over time, but naming the Washington football team the Redskins, we don't consider to be one of those bad things.[4]

Think about this for a minute: How many Indians do you see in government? How many do you see in politics? In entertainment? In sports? Not even enough to have a pow-wow. Team nicknames like

"Indians," "Fighting Sioux," and "Redskins" are forceful, popular reminders of Indian culture in America—and of Americans' respect for it. When Florida State football fans cheer on the Seminoles or Atlanta Braves fans do their tomahawk chop, the image in their minds is of courageous, fierce warriors—of something admirable, not an ethnic slur.

But not surprisingly, liberal sportscasters ignore the reality in front of them in preference to their holier-than-thou groupthink. Sports radio personality Dan Patrick had Bob Costas on his show the day after Costas derided the term Redskin as a "slur" and an "insult." Patrick said this:

> I think Daniel Snyder eventually changes the name. I don't know when, I just feel like there's an end game here.... I feel like he became his own worst enemy here by making it about him instead of being understanding about what it means, and who it affects. I don't want somebody to tell me how I'm supposed to think, and Daniel Snyder did that with Native Americans, and I think that's where people started to go wait a minute here. Nobody wants to be told what to think or what to do.[5]

Dan Snyder, of course, never told anyone what they had to think or do, nor did he make himself the story. He only made his own thinking perfectly clear when asked about the controversy, after the media tirade about "Redskins" being a racial slur. He told *USA Today*: "We will never change the name of the team. As a lifelong Redskins fan, and I think that the Redskins fans understand the great tradition and what it's all about and what it means...." He added, "We'll never change the name. It's that simple. NEVER—you can use caps."[6]

Dan Patrick is absolutely right on one thing: nobody wants to be told what to think or what to do, but that is *precisely* what he, Costas, and the rest of the liberal sports media have done and continue to do—you either agree with them or you're a racist. They're the ones who are pushing this non-issue as a story; they're the ones who insist on acting as thought police.

Why? Because you've got a bunch of sports guys who want to attach their names to something meaningful. After spending their entire careers covering seven-foot-six guys from China and twenty-one-year-olds who run sub-4.3 forties, inevitably they want to feel like their careers mean something, that they're socially relevant in some way, and the Redskins have become just that for the leftist sports media. Bob Costas and Peter King were not around when Jackie Robinson broke the color barrier in Major League Baseball. So the Redskins, to some extent, become their "Jackie Robinson" moment, and they will have that moment whether you want it or not.

Now, to be clear, I'm not trying to make an argument for keeping the Redskins' name. Yes, I grew up a fan of the team, and there's definitely some sentimentality there that makes me not want to see it changed. But if the Redskins changed their name to the Washington Silly Nannies, and started winning, and won a Super Bowl, I would be the Silliest Nanny of them all. My point is not that the Redskins' name is good or bad, but that this over-the-top, emotional push to drive the name Redskins from our sports lexicon did not materialize because "the people" are upset over it. The "people" don't really give a rip about what the Redskins call themselves, and if pressed, as they have been by the sports media, they would overwhelmingly prefer that the name stay the same and the sports media drop the subject.

But of course, the sports media aren't content to merely report and analyze sports news. They are not interested in informing and entertaining you; they want to reform and indoctrinate you. And that's a problem.

What's even more hilarious about the lefty sports crowd on the issue of Indian-themed sports nicknames is their inability to see the irony in their own irony. In 2002 a group of Indian college students at the University of Northern Colorado decided to name their intramural basketball team the Fightin' Whities in response to a local high school's team called the Fightin' Reds.

Apparently the students decided to print T-shirts as a way of sticking it to the paleface and making him taste the bitterness of his own racial medicine. The self-loathing palefaces in the sports media grabbed onto the Fightin' Whities story and, as usual, got it just about all wrong.

Keith Olbermann joined Paula Zahn and Anderson Cooper on CNN to praise the students' racial jiu-jitsu as "genius." Olbermann continued: "I think the point is being made here, how offensive this can be.... How the names that...we have grown up with—Indians, Braves, Redskins, Chiefs—how offensive they can be."[7]

Except that when Paula Zahn asked Olbermann to give examples of white people in Colorado offended by the Fightin' Whities, Olbermann couldn't come up with a single person. Instead, he waxed silly about the "attention" the issue had received nationally, and how it had put "people" (read: evil, treaty-breaking white people) in the position of the "offended party," which is the "best way to effect social change."[8]

But the real story was that no one was taking offense. White Coloradans did not consider themselves an offended party—they thought the name was funny or clever or anything but offensive. As syndicated columnist Clarence Page wrote, readers of the *Greeley Tribune* (the hometown paper of Eaton High School, where the Fightin' Reds nickname originated) wrote in to say they saw the nickname as "an honor to white Americans." One reader wrote in to say: "Help me out here, why am I supposed to be offended?"[9]

In fact, so epically did this little racial stunt fail to offend that Fightin' Whities T-shirts actually became a hot-selling item to the unoffended—so much so that the Native American Student Services office opened up the Fighting Whites Scholarship Fund with proceeds from the sales.

Ironic, isn't it? The would-be revolutionaries intent on showing whitey how cruel and demeaning it felt to be a mascot failed to offend anyone, and instead ended up selling T-shirts for the pale-faces' wampum.

And Northern Colorado intramural players weren't the only ones to go down this path. Shelf Life Clothing came up with a T-shirt that mocked the Chief Wahoo logo of the Cleveland Indians.[10] Instead of Chief Wahoo with the word "Indians" emblazoned above him, Shelf Life's creation had a blond-haired white guy in his place, a dollar sign where Wahoo's feather would normally sit, and "Caucasians" emblazoned above him.

The shirts have existed in relative obscurity for years, only recently coming into the spotlight when Ian Campeau, a DJ for a group called A Tribe Called Red, which includes three Ojibwa Indians, found himself called racist and hypocrite for wearing the shirt in publicity photos. You see, Campeau had previously filed a complaint with the Ontario Human Rights Commission to get a Canadian high school to change its team name from "Redskins" to "Eagles."

Campeau's publicity stunt paid off huge for Shelf Life. As the *Toronto Star* reported:

> A hot fashion item this summer on Ontario First Nations' reserves is a T-shirt with the lettering "Caucasians" and the grinning logo of Chief Wahoo, the much-derided mascot of the Cleveland Indians major league baseball team.... T-shirt maker Brian Kirby of Shelf Life Clothing in Cleveland said the "Caucasians" shirt has been his most popular seller since he began making them in 2007, but interest "skyrocketed" after the Deejay NDN (Ian Campeau) controversy, especially after the story hit Reddit and Facebook.[11]

NBC Sports' HardballTalk.com's Craig Calcaterra greeted news of the T-shirt's success with sarcastic glee: "I've been told by so many people that, in reality, no one cares about Chief Wahoo, most Indians feel 'honored' by their images and iconography being appropriated by sports teams and that the politics of race and sports mascots is purely a function of liberal white guilt and pinkos like me wishing to push our agenda. Hmm. Guess not."[12]

Uh, Craig, guess again. If the intent of the shirt was to offend white Americans or white Cleveland Indians fans, it failed utterly. Again, people weren't offended: they thought the T-shirts were funny, which is why demand exploded. Most Americans still have a life, a sense of humor, and better things to do than obsess over team nicknames. Most Americans, in this case, would not include sports reporters. In fact, if the Caucasians and Fightin' Whities T-shirts proved anything, it is that many Americans will buy a shirt that they see as *making fun of people offended by team nicknames, or as making fun of the sports media's racial obsessions.*

The hypocrisy and stupidity of media coverage of the Redskins is not limited to T-shirt sales and *Sunday Night Football* monologues.

In October 2014, a Fox broadcast of the Redskins versus Cardinals game in Phoenix showed Redskins owner Daniel Snyder sitting alongside Navajo Nation president Ben Shelly. It gets better. Shelly and his wife each wore Redskins hats.

The excrement storm that followed on social media was completely predictable. Here are some of the more memorable Twitter contributions to the highbrow discourse:

> Jess @JessOfRVA: Dan Snyder is parading around the President of the Navajo nation in Redskins Gear. Good Lord.
> Maya @pho_re: @5150ellis #dansnyder is parading these people like property with little hats #disgusting.

And last but certainly not least . . .

> Alex Hale @DaSportsGenius7: Wait the President of the Navajo Nation is in Dan Snyder's suite? Now if only Cartman was there to say, "Washington Redskins go F yourself."

(Side note: Do you see how these liberals refer to the Navajo president as being "paraded" around by Snyder, as if he's a non-thinking person without any free will whatsoever? If you ever want to see what liberals truly think of minorities, wait until a minority goes against them on a political or cultural issue. You'll see libs go from hippy-dippy lover of all the earth's creatures to racists of a sort that would make Bull Connor cringe. But they get away with it because, you know, they're uber-tolerant . . . or something.)

The backlash to Shelly's solidarity with Snyder, though, wasn't confined to mouth-breathers in their pajamas. The mouth-breathers in the sports media got in on the act real quick. Right after the television image of Snyder and Shelly appeared, ESPN's Bomani Jones tweeted this gem: "dude in the box with snyder was also once accused of stealing from the nation. he was cleared, but check the details."[13]

First of all, funny how quickly the president of the Navajo Nation gets demoted to "dude" when sitting next to the owner of the Redskins, isn't it? That "dude" has a lot more credibility on the issue of the Redskins' name change than Bomani Jones or any other member of the leftist sports media by virtue of his being not only an Indian, but also an actual leader of Indians. But here he ran afoul of the stated sports media agenda, thus rendering himself merely a dude.

The link in Jones's tweet described a sordid affair in which the Navajo president settled out of court after accusations that he stole more than $8,850 from the tribal government. Ben Shelly, the Navajo president, adamantly maintained his innocence of theft. He returned all of the money, except for $600, which Shelly had used to bury his mother. The judge in the case dismissed the charges.

Deadspin also fired off a tweet about Shelly soon after he appeared next to Snyder, linking to an article charitably titled "Disgraced, Soon-to-Be-Former Navajo Nation President Attends Skins Game."[14] As Daniel Flynn described it at Breitbart.com, "The sports site, suddenly expert on tribal politics, maintains that the Navajo Nation president 'entered office under a dark cloud' and 'was accused of going behind the back of tribal leaders.' The only good Indian is a *Deadspin* Indian."[15]

And that's not all they said. *Deadspin* went on to provide in-depth detail of Shelly's recent election loss and past conflicts with the tribal councils, which is fine. I'm not here to defend Ben Shelly. But I do think his willingness to openly support the Redskins as an Indian man of some stature—whether on his way in or out of power—is important and should be taken seriously. I do know that neither *Deadspin* nor any other branch of the left-wing media machine went to such lengths to do "opposition research" on any of the Indians who *support* the Redskins' name change.

When Ray Halbritter, leader of the Oneida tribe, emerged as the most vocal Indian leader of the Change the Mascot movement, *Deadspin* had only very vague references to his background. *Deadspin* writer Dave McKenna, for instance, described Halbritter as an "Oneida Indian frontman."[16] Sean Newell, also writing for *Deadspin*, referred to Halbritter as an "Oneida Indian Nation Representative."[17]

If *Deadspin* had done the same sort of oppo research on Halbritter as they had done on Ben Shelly, they would have found some significant stories. For example, according to a report by the Christian Peacemaker Teams, Ray Halbritter cemented himself as head of the Oneida tribe by building a casino.

> In 1993, Mr. Halbritter negotiated a gaming compact for the Oneidas with New York governor Mario Cuomo.... This casino became the cornerstone of an expansive Oneida business enterprise that now includes a chain of gas stations, a textile factory, and a luxury hotel. The business is incorporated as the Oneida Indian Nation of New York, Inc. with Ray Halbritter as its CEO.[18]

As Daniel Greenfield of FrontPageMag.com pithily summed it up: "So yes, Ray Halbritter is a representative of the Oneida Indian Nation. But it's the Oneida Indian Nation Inc. It's a company with gas stations, a hotel, and a casino."[19]

It gets better:

> In 1993, the Grand Council of Chiefs removed Mr. Hal-
> britter as the Oneida wolf clan representative and notified
> the federal Bureau of Indian Affairs (BIA) that he no longer
> represented the Oneida people. The decision was accepted
> by the BIA, only to be reversed 24 hours later, reportedly
> under pressure from Sherwood Boehlert, the U.S. congres-
> sional representative for the area and a casino supporter.
>
> Today the U.S. government but not the Grand Council
> of Chiefs gives official recognition to the Oneida Indian
> Nation with Ray Halbritter as its representative.[20]

So Ray Halbritter is not even considered a legitimate representative by his own people! Who is it that considers him legitimate? The
white man! The palefaces in Washington!

And it gets better still:

> On February 13, 1996, the Center for Constitutional
> Rights (CCR) and local counsel filed suit on behalf of the
> Oneida Nation of New York against the U.S. Department
> of the Interior, charging that the government violated the
> Oneidas' national sovereignty.
>
> The suit alleged that the Department refused to recog-
> nize a legitimate decision by the Nation and the Grand
> Council of the Haudenosaunee, Six Nations Confederacy,
> to remove Arthur Raymond Halbritter from his claimed
> position as sole leader of the Nation and representative to
> the U.S. government.[21]

Here you have the Indian people actually suing the federal government to have this clown removed, and why? Because, as the Oneidas protested:

> Against the wishes of the Confederacy, and without knowledge of the Oneida people, a Casino deal was struck between ex-Governor Cuomo and so-called Oneida Nation "CEO" Arthur Raymond Halbritter in 1993. The compact was never ratified by the Oneidas. Using money borrowed by Halbritter from the Key Bank of Central NY (the CEO mortgaged Oneida land without our knowledge) "The Turning Stone Casino" was built in Oneida, NY. The Casino was built on wetlands in violation of both US and Haudenosaunee laws. Because Halbritter violated Haudenosaunee rules he was removed from his position as an Oneida spokesperson in May, 1993....
>
> The Oneida people were completely unaware that any transactions for land, a casino, or lawsuits against 20,000 land owners would ensue. To date, the Oneida people who have opposed these decisions continue to be threatened with on-going human, civil and religious rights violations and are in present danger of losing their homes on the Oneida Indian Territory. Under the guise of a "beautification program", the leadership has authorized a mock tribal court system to prosecute all those who stand up for their rights as Haudenosaunee. A 54 man, completely non-Native "Oneida Nation Police" force acting on the direct orders of Halbritter has harassed, intimidated and physically assaulted Oneida people on their own territory.[22]

In short, Ray Halbritter built himself a casino empire against the wishes of his own people and then hired a goon squad to make sure they stayed in line. But why do we have to find all this information out from FrontPageMag.com and OneidasforDemocracy.org? Where was *Deadspin* on this? The answer to that, of course, is that the liberal media do opposition research against people whose beliefs they don't like, but they will give a pretty much free ride to those who toe the liberal party line.

Ben Shelly *might* have wrongfully taken less than $9,000 from his tribe, and more than 90 percent of that money he returned. Yet *Deadspin* saw fit to call him a "disgraced," "soon-to-be-former President" and a "lame duck" who had entered office under a "dark cloud."

Forget a lame duck, Ray Halbritter is a dead duck with the Oneida. He was voted out twenty years ago, yet, thanks to the U.S. government, he still spends Oneida money and uses that money to hire goons who have assaulted tribal people. Because he chooses to let the Left use him as a true "mascot" in their quest to remove all Indian mascots, *Deadspin* sees fit to refer to him only as a "frontman" and a "representative."

The Redskins' trip to Arizona in 2014 wasn't just about what we saw on TV, with Navajo president Ben Shelly sitting next to Daniel Snyder. It was also about what we didn't see. The great website RedskinsFacts.com—which dedicates itself to getting out the truth about the Redskins' name—continuously tweeted pictures of dozens of Indians wearing Redskins jerseys, proudly waving signs in support of the name, and posing for pictures with famous former Redskins like Mark Moseley and Gary Clark.

I give Fox full credit for showing Ben Shelly with Daniel Snyder. But if it were not for RedskinsFacts.com, few of us would know just how deep and widespread is the Redskins' support among American

Indians. That's not something the liberal sports media want you to know.

Think of it this way: If these Indians had wanted the Redskins to change their name, would they have received more attention and airtime? You bet they would have.

When it comes to the liberal sports media, sports reporter Daniel Flynn of Breitbart.com nailed it: "The only good Indian is a *Deadspin* Indian."

CHAPTER FOUR

MAKING A HERO
OF MICHAEL SAM

I normally don't watch local news. The mullet-to-secondary-education ratio is far too imbalanced for me; for some reason, local television news is completely obsessed with covering the decay of Western society. Occasionally I see a quality story and solid journalistic work, but normally within three minutes of watching, I feel like I'm witnessing the news equivalent of the primordial ooze river from *Ghostbusters II*. So with great fear, trepidation, and yet some semblance of hope, I turned on my local Fox affiliate here in Houston to get an update on the Rockets. I, like a true NBA fan when his team goes out of time zone, had fallen asleep during their game against Phoenix the night before, and I wanted to see the highlights.

After wading through a seemingly endless myriad of "Woman Shoots Baby-Daddy for Farting Too Loud" and "Dog Finds Car Keys in Baby's Diaper" stories (not literally, but you know what I'm talking about), the NBA coverage began. However, instead of coverage of the team that…you know…plays for the city in which the television station's audience lives, I found myself treated to a highlight montage of Jason Collins, who had recently announced that he had sex with men—in other words, was gay—which was treated as an act of national importance and tremendous heroism. Here he was, playing in the first game since his coming out. The montage was set to the tune of John Lennon's "Imagine."

"'Imagine' what?" a viewer might have asked. Certainly not what Jason Collins got up to in his alleged private life, now made public. Moreover, why would a local television station that airs in Houston, Texas, a place where Jason Collins never played in his career, instead of airing coverage of the team they "cover" (and a team that won that night in Phoenix, by the way), choose to go with a heavily produced tribute piece about a thirty-five-year-old journeyman basketball player, playing in Los Angeles for a team from Brooklyn?

Well, we all know the answer. Because when it comes to sports media, if it's gay, it leads.

Now, this chapter is going to deal primarily with the Michael Sam story as opposed to Jason Collins for a few reasons. First, Michael Sam is more recent, and he also plays in the biggest sports league in America, the NFL. And on a personal level, I have to say, even though I have about as much interest in hearing about the sex life of another man as I have in chewing glass, I respect Michael Sam and the way he came out much more than I respect the way Jason Collins did.

Michael Sam came out at the *beginning* of his career, before the draft even. Jason Collins came out after the last game of what absolutely should have been his last season. It's one thing to shout, "I'm gay!" as you're leaving a party. It's quite another to shout it out as you're entering one. Trust me on this.

After Jason Collins announced he was homosexual, at the end of the 2013 NBA season, he was not signed to another NBA contract. Some people (ESPN) believe this was done for anti-gay reasons, and that it looked awful for the league to have a player publicly come out, only to have nobody sign him.

Other people (non-gay-rights advocates, using their brains) know that no team came within ten yards of Jason Collins at the end of the 2013 season, because he wasn't the same player anymore. In the 2012–2013 season, Collins had played in only 38 games, logged only 384 minutes, and been held to 41 points and 60 rebounds over that time. If you put up those stats at twenty-four while bouncing between an NBA team and the Development League, *maybe* a team sticks with you and tries to bring you around. But when you do that at thirty-four, the party's over. So Jason Collins remained unemployed— that is, until University of Missouri defensive end Michael Sam announced to the world in February 2014 that he was gay too, thus sparking the strangest race in the history of history: "The Great Gay Race" of 2014.

Not to be outdone by the NFL, the NBA moved quickly. Exactly two weeks after Michael Sam made his announcement, Jason Collins signed a ten-day contract with the Brooklyn Nets and played the very next night. If you needed any proof that Jason Collins was signed only because he was gay, take a look at his stat line: in his first game back, against the Lakers, Collins played eleven minutes and logged two rebounds (rebounding had previously been his strength). He missed his only field-goal attempt and committed *five fouls*. That is the stat line of someone who has no business being on an NBA basketball court. More important, any prospect from the NBA's Development League could have done as well, or better, and so could a lot of other free-agent veterans. Jason Collins was signed purely because he was gay and it helped the NBA and the Nets make a political statement to the adoring liberal sports media. Having a gay player proves that you're a tolerant, nuanced, open-minded, and loving human being. Not having one means that you're hateful, "behind the times," and cruel to small woodland creatures. Professional sports leagues are keenly aware that gay activism has become the new liberal cause célèbre, and they want to be at its forefront.

It was absurd to ask, as the liberal sports media did repeatedly, whether the NBA or the NFL was ready for a gay athlete, because everyone knew there had been gay athletes before (though they had kept it private) and everyone knew there would be no quicker way to fawning media coverage than to have an openly gay player. That's why the NBA snatched Jason Collins off Oprah's couch in February 2014 and threw an NBA uniform on him—because he was gay and it made the NBA and the Nets look good, at least in the eyes of the sports media.

The NBA may have won the battle of "The Great Gay Race," but the NFL will win the war, because the NFL is the NFL. Michael Sam is the big one: an NFL player playing the country's most popular game. The sports media greeted the Michael Sam announcement with jubilation unparalleled. *Sports Illustrated*'s Stewart Mandel wrote about how Sam had broken "a longstanding barrier."[1] NFL Network analyst Mark Kriegel tweeted: "Mizzou's Michael Sam just showed people what it's like to be a real man."[2] *Grantland* staff writer Holly Anderson tweeted: "The support from Michael Sam's teammates puts gladness in my heart. Bless them all."[3] Rob Moseley of GoDucks.com tweeted: "The Michael Sam news is massive, groundbreaking—and long overdue—stuff. Awesome for him, and for those who will follow in his footsteps."[4] Will Brinson, senior writer for CBS Sports, said,

"So much for Johnny Manziel having the biggest crowd at the combine. Incredibly brave decision by Michael Sam."[5]

Now, sportswriters are supposed to know something about the meaning of words, and all of the words above are a prime, grade-A bullfeathers. Contrary to Stewart Mandel, Sam had not broken a longstanding barrier, because there was no covert or overt rule against gay athletes in the NFL. If for Mark Kriegel the definition of a real man is someone who talks about his sex life, well, that seems a pretty impoverished view, and I wonder if he would take the same view if an athlete said he intended to remain a virgin until he got married. New York Giants cornerback Prince Amukamara did that and was roundly ridiculed for it. I wonder how often Holly Anderson "blesses" football players—isn't it funny or ironic how sportswriters use words of religion or morality to approve behavior that used to be considered neither religious nor moral? Rob Moseley thought the Sam news was "massive, groundbreaking," while most sports fans probably thought the news was something more akin to "thanks for sharing." And as for what Will Brinson calls the "incredibly brave decision" by Michael Sam, how incredibly brave is it to make an announcement that any PR person could tell you would suddenly make you a hero in the eyes of the sports media, and even merit—as did the Jason Collins announcement—a congratulatory phone call or statement of support from the president of the United States? Just as an aside, can you imagine previous presidents considering a man's announcement that he has sex with other men worthy of presidential commendation—George Washington congratulating the first openly gay Indian lacrosse player, or Abraham Lincoln congratulating the first openly gay jockey, or FDR congratulating the first openly gay race car driver?

It's instructive to compare the sports media's treatment of Heisman Trophy winner Tim Tebow when he was drafted in the first round with their treatment of seventh-round draft pick Michael Sam. You can guess who got the easier ride. Pete Prisco of CBS Sports referred to Tebow's pro day at Florida as "St. Timmy's Day."[6] He trashed Tebow's NFL potential and even wondered whether Tebow was charging for pictures (he wasn't). Prisco made a cottage industry of anti-Tebow columns, concluding that Tebow "stinks," might have "learning problems," and was "not a great teammate."[7] Others were even less forgiving, and blunter. Jeff Pearlman of *Sports Illustrated* left little doubt where he stood on "Saint Timmy" when he wrote a blog post titled "I Want Tim Tebow to Fail."[8] Imagine the reaction if a sports writer had written an article titled "I Want Michael Sam to Fail." That writer would have been fired—and then probably loaded into a cannon and fired into the polar vortex. There would have been universal outrage.

But there was no such outrage at Jeff Pearlman, who in that blog post said everything that the liberal sports media thought needed to be said:

> I want him to fail in the NFL nonetheless, because a famous Tim Tebow is a dangerous Tim Tebow. Tim Tebow scares me and judging from his father's website, his upcoming Super Bowl ad and mounting knowledge of his way of life he should scare you, too. Tim Tebow doesn't play football merely for the joy of the game. He plays football because he wants to spread the word of Jesus Christ.[9]

Yeah, all that "turn the other cheek," "love thy neighbor," and saving unwanted children in Philippines stuff? Horrifying.

And while Pearlman wanted Tebow to fail because Tebow is a devout evangelical Christian, Pearlman (who is Jewish) *gushed* over Brooklyn-based Orthodox Jewish fighter Dmitriy Salita who also goes by the nickname "The Star of David." In another blog post, Pearlman describes Salita as being "genuinely pious."[10] But, despite the fact that Salita is essentially the Jewish Tim Tebow, Pearlman never said he wants Salita to fail. On the contrary, Pearlman even went on to call Salita his favorite "Jewish jock"[11] of all time. So it's okay for a Jewish fighter to be openly devout, but it's not okay for a Christian athlete? And of course when Michael Sam announced that he was going to be the first openly gay NFL player, Pearlman gushed again:

> Michael Sam is my new favorite football player.
>
> I don't have a close second....
>
> ...Some teammates will avoid him in the showers. There'll be whispers and chuckles. Religious teammates will damn him a sinner. Maybe to his face, maybe not. But the words, they will speak.
>
> And yet...I get the feeling this man can take it. He's clearly intelligent and insightful. He braved coming out to his college teammates, and was encouraged by the aftermath. He seems to know he's a trailblazer; seems comfortable carrying that torch.
>
> I've never seen him play, but I expect my son to be wearing his jersey next season.
>
> With pride.[12]

Okay, so Michael Sam is Pearlman's "new favorite football player," and he doesn't have "a close second," even though he's "never seen him play." In other words, Sam is Pearlman's favorite player *solely because* Sam is openly gay, and Pearlman is rooting for Sam to succeed just as he rooted for Tebow to fail, because Tebow "wants to spread the word of Christ" while Sam is "a trailblazer" carrying the "torch" of gay activism, and the sports media love the latter and loathe the former.

But as giddy and jubilant as the sports media were after Michael Sam's announcement that he was gay, there was still a problem. No one else seemed to care. All the supposedly racist, homophobic religious zealots were remarkably quiet. Dave Zirin, sports editor for the very liberal magazine the *Nation*, was even moved to write an article that posed the question: "Why the Curious Right-Wing Silence on Michael Sam?"[13]

I don't know, maybe it's because the rest of the country isn't as obsessed with homosexuality as sports columnists are, and maybe most people have better things to do than talk about the sex lives of others. The sports media were perplexed that the "right wing" appeared far less "homophobic" than advertised. So how did the sports media handle this? Extensions of friendships? Apologies? Back rubs? Long walks on the beach? No, they decided to pick a fight.

Dale Hansen, a sports anchor for WFAA television in Dallas, couldn't resist, as almost all liberal sportscasters can't resist, the idea that gay is the new black:

> It wasn't that long ago when we were being told that black players couldn't play in "our" games because it would be "uncomfortable." And even when they finally could, it took several more years before a black man played quarterback.
>
> Because we weren't "comfortable" with that, either.

So many of the same people who used to make that argument (and the many who still do) are the same people who say government should stay out of our lives.

But then want government in our bedrooms.

I've never understood how they feel "comfortable" laying claim to both sides of that argument.[14]

Hansen's thinking is so confused here I have almost no idea what he's really trying to say. But, I'll give it a try. It seems like Hansen is blaming small-government types, in other words, Republicans, and Christian Republicans in particular—you know, the ones who support small government *and* traditional morality—for the color bar that used to keep professional sports segregated. And I guess he's saying that these same people opposed black quarterbacks and now oppose Michael Sam. Make sense? Maybe if you're Bob Costas or Keith Olbermann; otherwise, Hansen's whole rant is beyond silly, as is his final slap at Republicans' "wanting government in our bedrooms." Really? Like when? I thought it was liberals who were responsible for putting, on the taxpayers' dime, the "bedroom" stuff in our public schools, including all sorts of LGBT (lesbian, gay, bisexual, and transgender) propaganda; Obamacare, which has made us pay for everyone else's contraception (more bedroom stuff); the liberal welfare state that has made us pay for everyone else's abortions, STDs, and illegitimate children (yet more bedroom stuff); and the Obama administration's inclusion of gay liberation as part of our foreign policy, flying the LGBT rainbow flag from some of our embassies, or in other words having the government take the sheets out of certain bedrooms and fly them on a flagpole representing our nation.

But back to sports. Let's begin with some facts. Branch Rickey, the Dodgers executive who decided to snatch Jackie Robinson out of relative obscurity and shatter baseball's color barrier by bringing him up to the big leagues with the Brooklyn Dodgers, was, wait for it, a Republican. In fact, so was Jackie Robinson until the late 1960s, when he supported Hubert Humphrey for president. And guess what? Both men were devout Christians.

As for the first black quarterback to win a Super Bowl, that was Doug Williams, and his head coach was a Christian conservative Republican named Joe Gibbs. The same Joe Gibbs who spoke at the 2008 Republican National Convention, and the same Joe Gibbs who benched a white quarterback named Jay Schroeder in order to give Williams the starting job that he had rightfully earned. Not to mention that Jack Kent Cooke, who was the Redskins owner at the time and the boss of both Williams and Gibbs, was also a staunch Republican.

Hansen wants to imply that Republicans—those small-government, moralistic types—are racists. But the inconvenient truth for Hansen is that it was Republicans who broke the color barrier in baseball, it was Republicans who gave us the first black quarterback to win a Super Bowl, and it was Republicans who were saying next to nothing about Michael Sam at the time that Hansen decided to go on his rant.

Hansen loosed his tirade after some anonymous NFL executives and personnel types told *Sports Illustrated* that Sam's announcement could hurt his draft stock.[15] So naturally Hansen took the assessment of NFL executives and scouts as a means to attack conservatives for being, guess what, racist and for wanting to get into your bedroom. Makes sense, doesn't it? Well, it does if you're in sports media. Or any mainstream media for that matter. After Sam was drafted and was filmed kissing his boyfriend, an anchor named Courtney Kerr on a

Dallas morning TV show called *The Broadcast* said that critical comments about Sam's messy display of affection were "racist toward homosexuals."[16] Her coanchor Lisa Pineiro, a fellow liberal, actually attacked conservatives for *not* wanting to hear or see more stories about Michael Sam. People were, she said, and she implied that she was one of them, "very sick of people who are being sick of hearing about [Michael Sam stories]."[17] There we have a point-blank confession that conservatives might not want to talk obsessively about gays, but the liberal media sure do.

Since they couldn't get much of a rise with the Michael Sam coming-out story, they tried, and partly succeeded, by airing or posting, around the clock, video or pictures of Michael Sam kissing his boyfriend. Has an NFL draft pick's public display of affection ever been more widely aired? For the sports and mainstream media, it was as iconic as that end-of-World-War-II picture of a sailor kissing a nurse in Times Square. Even better, the liberal sports media knew it was offending the instincts and sentiments of a lot of people who are willing to tolerate homosexuality but don't want it broadcast into their living room or to their children who, you know, watch sports media for sports, not the national gay lip-locking championship. It's not conservatives who want government in the bedroom—handing out "free" contraception à la Obamacare—but rather the liberal sports media, broadcasting gay kissing into every electronic device you might have in your bedroom.

And if you're a professional football player who happens to tweet "horrible" and "OMG"[18] at the spectacle, as Miami Dolphins safety Don Jones did, don't expect any sympathy from the sports media after the team fines you, suspends you, and sends you to "educational training," because these journalists are perfectly fine with what the Communists used to call "reeducation camps."

The liberal sports media think gay rights are a civil rights crusade and those who think otherwise need to have their thinking changed, which is why it is "racist" not to want round-the-clock coverage of Michael Sam kissing his boyfriend, why the liberal sports media think they are so bravely progressive when they broadcast it, and why the liberal sports media will fall right behind NFL management in stifling any dissent on this issue.

For the sports media, the enemy is always the same: conservatives and Christians. The "ground" the liberal sports media want to break is the ground of traditional Christian morality. Shortly after Jason Collins came out, the *Washington Post*'s Mike Wise waxed stupid about those he felt were opposed to Collins. He, cowardly, did not name, though he paraphrased, ESPN NBA analyst Chris Broussard, who was pretty much the only member of the sports media to be openly critical of Collins, citing homosexuality as an "open rebellion against God."[19] Wise quickly went to full froth as he attacked the "heterosexual religious zealots" who "used [Collins's] historic announcement to call homosexuality a sin and an open rebellion toward God and otherwise trumpeted their bigotry under the guise of 'religious beliefs.'"[20]

In other words, if Christians consider homosexuality a sin, then they are bigots. Not much liberal tolerance for Christians, is there? Wise continued: "Let's at least be consistent: If the outrage at Collins is all about religion, where was the contempt for Shawn Kemp's and Antonio Cromartie's serial fathering? Really, why is an openly gay athlete evoking such fervor while a womanizing athlete is just one of the fellas?"[21]

There are a couple of points to be made here. First, there wasn't a lot of outrage—in fact, there was hardly any—at Jason Collins's announcement. There was no anti-Collins "fervor." The fervor was all on the side of the liberal sports media, who trumpeted a story that very few people cared about and lashed out against "bigots" who were almost entirely silent, perhaps even nearly nonexistent. If you looked at any sports media blog, you'd quickly find that most any "outrage" was directed not at Collins but at the sports media's endless clamor about Collins, which is why sports media liberals were "very sick of people who are being sick of hearing about it," as Lisa Pineiro said about Michael Sam.

And as for the lack of "contempt for Shawn Kemp's and Antonio Cromartie's serial fathering," is it really the role of Christians to show contempt for anyone? Christians are called to charity, and it's telling that Wise doesn't know that—contempt seems to be more his line when he talks about Christians.

Speaking as a sports commentator, I can tell you that the real reason sports writers steer away from talking about athletes and their "baby mamas" is because they don't want to be called *racist*. Mike Wise knows this. Whenever someone criticizes a Kemp or a Cromartie for his "serial fathering," he gets shouted down and vilified. Case in point was when, in 2013, one of NFL running back Adrian Peterson's *many* illegitimate children was tragically beaten to death by a monster whom the child's mother was living with. Phil Mushnick, a sports writer for the *New York Post*, then took Peterson to task. Mushnick was angry with Peterson for not providing a better home for his son and for living a lifestyle that made his kids vulnerable because he wasn't there to be a father for them, saying:

> Maybe Peterson's son is just one more stands-to-reason murder victim, just another child born to just another "baby mama," one more kid who never had a shot, anyway. Maybe, by now, even if we can't accept it, we can

expect it.... The suspect in the beating murder of Peterson's 2-year-old is the boyfriend of Peterson's "baby mama"— now the casual, flippant, detestable and common buzz-phrase for absentee, wham-bam fatherhood.[22]

And for those comments, Mushnick was ripped by the sports media. *Deadspin* described Mushnick as a "professional shithead" and "race-baiting troll."[23] The site Awful Announcing called Mushnick's piece "the most offensive sports column in the history of Earth."[24] It is Wise's fellow travelers in the liberal sports media, who are quick to yell racism and quick to reject Christian morality, who make it nearly impossible to criticize athletes for impregnating their serial baby mamas.

Wise saved the kicker for the end: "Collins being gay is about him, not anyone else. By sharing his sexual identity publicly, he's stating who *he* is, not what anyone else should be."[25]

Yeah, and that's why you're writing about it in one of the country's largest newspapers, and that's why the Collins and the Sam stories dominated ESPN for days, because all this is a private moment for Jason Collins and Michael Sam. Please. I could have said the exact same thing about Tim Tebow. Tebow's Christianity was about him, and not necessarily anyone else. He opened the door to others who might want to follow, but he in no way compelled them to or damned them if they didn't. So what's the difference? The sports media like what Sam stands for and loathe what Tebow stands for.

This moment ceased having anything to do with Jason Collins the second he said, "I'm gay." Collins was just the means to an end for the liberal sports media. As Matt Philbin of the Media Research Center said, Collins is their "gay Jackie Robinson."[26] Collins and Sam might say they just want to play ball and don't want to be activists, and that's fine. But it doesn't matter. The sports media will turn them into activists. That same sports media, however, could also be their undoing. In a moment of breathtaking honesty, Gregg Doyel of CBS Sports tweeted out an article that he wrote, with the catch line in the tweet reading: "Michael Sam and the liberal media: Match made in heaven, or...not?"[27]

Hats off to Gregg Doyel for acknowledging that the liberal media are...the liberal media. He goes further:

> The media wants Michael Sam to succeed. I could ignore that and write something else about him, something that would sound very much like I want him to succeed—and I do, unabashedly and unapologetically—but ignoring the obvious is no way to go through life. So let's not ignore that Michael Sam has fans in newsrooms and press boxes around the country.
>
> See, Michael Sam is a story, one we've been waiting on for years. We in the national media have long anticipated a publicly gay male professional athlete in one of our biggest sports leagues—the NFL, MLB, the NBA—and we almost had one last year when Jason Collins came out. The media fawned over Collins' announcement, and I could pretend that didn't happen but it's like I've already said: Ignoring the facts is no way to go through life. Hell, I was fawning myself. Unabashedly and unapologetically.
>
> So the mostly liberal media has a story that we find not just fascinating, but inspiring. And we're going to write about Michael Sam as much as we can, as I'm doing right here, because it's so fun and new and progressive.

NFL teams will be watching, reading. And at some
point you have to wonder if the overexposure that killed the
career of Tim Tebow will do the same to Michael Sam.[28]

Now, first off, the obvious difference between Sam and Tebow is
that the media actually *wanted* Tim Tebow to fail. They viewed him,
his family, and what he stood for as a clear and present danger to what
they believe, and they wanted him gone. If Michael Sam's NFL career
face-plants after a year or two because of the "media circus," it will
be sad, and no doubt some of those liberals in those press boxes and
newsrooms will lament the tragic downfall they helped to make happen. But, in the end, Michael Sam's career demise would just be col-
lateral damage. The sports media don't care about Michael Sam. They
care about what Michael Sam represents. As Doyel says, this is the
story "we've been waiting on for years."

And that's sad. What's also sad is that so many reporters were
waiting on this for so long. Why? What's such a big deal about a kid
being gay and playing football? What would it prove? What kind of
warped mind-set do you have to be in to lose sleep at night wondering
when and whence the first gay football player is coming? More important, why weren't they waiting for someone like Tebow? With all the
domestic violence, rapes, murders, broken homes, bankruptcy, and
other crap that the sports world produces nowadays, if you were going
to lose sleep over waiting for a great story and a breath of fresh air,
wouldn't you have been hoping for a Tim Tebow? Instead, your answer
to all of that was to anxiously anticipate the first gay player? What
does that say about the people who are bringing you your sports news?

Unfortunately, what it offers is more evidence that gay activism
has become the new religion of the sports media. Sports have always
taken relatively obscure players like Michael Sam and Jason Collins

and helped turn them into heroes. But, in the past, that kind of hero- or icon-making was reserved for people who had either done incredible things on the field of play or done incredibly brave and heroic things away from the field of play. Michael Sam and Jason Collins can lay claim to no such exploits on the playing field. Their icon stature is due solely to their homosexuality and the "bravery" they showed in coming out.

But what's brave or heroic about saying you're gay in America in 2014? Not much. The fact is, coming out has become, as Matt Philbin of the Media Research Center describes it, more about joining "society's most trendy and celebrated grievance group."[29] All it means is that *Sports Center* is going to be showing your highlights all day, Oprah's booking agent will be calling soon, and you're probably going to pick up about thirty thousand Twitter followers. I'm not saying coming out doesn't require a certain degree of self-confidence. But bravery? What's brave in America in 2014 is going to Radio Row at the Super Bowl and telling someone you voted for Romney.

I don't have anything against Michael Sam personally. I've got enough trouble keeping up with my own sex life, let alone his or anyone else's. But I have to say I really do wish they would keep it to themselves. Few of us feel the need to talk about our sex lives. Most of us think there is a lot more to us than what we do behind closed doors. But the only reason we're asked to know or care about Jason Collins or Michael Sam is because they're gay, and that's a problem.

I should know about you because of *what* you've done, not because of *whom* you've done. Are we really getting to a point in society where people are known and identified by whom they go horizontal with?

It seems like we are, and whether you're gay or straight, that's not a good thing.

Especially, and bizarrely, when having a Christian point of view on these issues can cost you your job.

That's how liberals play the "tolerance" game. It's a matter of definition: they're tolerant, and you're not; and because you're not, you might get sued or lose your job or be otherwise publicly vilified.

David Tyree found this out firsthand. In 2014, the New York Giants decided to hire their former wide receiver and Super Bowl XLII hero as director of player development.

Tyree had previously spoken publicly about his views on gay marriage. According to Breitbart.com:

> In 2011 Tyree got involved in the campaign in New York on the question of same-sex marriage and said same-sex marriage would lead to "anarchy." He maintained, "The nuclear family is the backbone of society," "marriage existed prior to our country," and "redefining marriage changes everything including the way we educate our children."
>
> "This is not personal," the sure-handed receiver explained. "I could still be in a locker room with a gay man and still love him as a teammate. I can be tolerant, but the problem is people aren't tolerant of the views people like me have. If you don't agree with that lifestyle, you're a bigot. I'm not a bigot. I have different viewpoints."[30]

As if on cue, to ensure that Tyree's statement on intolerance completely fulfilled the prophecy, the benignly named but liberally inspired Human Rights Campaign attacked Tyree. The HRC called his beliefs "misinformed and dangerous."[31] What seemed to annoy the HRC at first was Tyree's statement that he would trade his Super Bowl win for a society that maintains the institution of traditional marriage: "As a player, David Tyree made clear that his misguided personal views trump his responsibility to his teammates and his employer."[32]

Good. I'm glad David Tyree's personal views and strongly held convictions trump his responsibility to his employer. They should. How strongly or dearly held is a personal view or conviction if it can be overruled by the guy signing your paycheck?

David Tyree had a good NFL career. The only reason he is a household name to millions of sports fans is because of his amazing circus catch that helped make the Giants' win in Super Bowl XLII possible. That Super Bowl and that moment will likely become the only thing that people remember from his playing career; and yet, he would trade away that signature moment of his career for traditional marriage. Good for him.

You would think that in a sane world, the HRC and others of their ilk could have at least felt a begrudging respect for the depth of his commitment, his sense of principle, even if they disagreed with him. Instead, the only depths the HRC managed to go to were name-calling and fearmongering.

Tyree really got under their skin with his strong belief in gay conversion. As Tyree said in a 2011 Twitter exchange on the civil rights and gay rights movements: "I'll never be a former black. I have met former homosexuals."[33]

It was this that led to the hissiest of all hissy-fit responses from the HRC:

> "When did Tyree decide to be straight?" Human Rights Campaign president Chad Griffin asked in a statement criticizing the Giants for hiring the former receiver. "The idea that someone can change their sexual orientation or

gender identity is ludicrous and the New York Giants are risking their credibility by hiring someone who publicly advocates junk science. His opposition to basic legal equality aside, David Tyree's proselytizing of such dangerous practices goes against the positive work the Giants organization has done in recent years."[34]

Gay conversion equals kryptonite to PC police and activists like the HRC. It's the one thing they can't allow over and above all else. It's not "science" that these activists are pushing; it's an agenda defended by intimidation, intolerance, and even, in some states, the force of law. The readily observable fact that gays walk away from, and heteros walk into, homosexuality every year brings *their* junk-science, "it's not a choice" house of cards crashing down. The fact that David Tyree publicly expressed that fact with his simple yet forceful take about meeting former homosexuals yet never having met former blacks became good enough to get him marked for figurative death.

But reports of Tyree's career death were greatly exaggerated. The Giants went ahead and made the hire. David Tyree also tried to appease the homosexual lobby that wanted to kill his career by meeting with Wade Davis, the executive director of the You Can Play foundation, which aims to eliminate "homophobia."

The *New York Daily News* reported that You Can Play cofounder Patrick Burke released a tweet suggesting that Tyree was "evolving" in his views. Not only that, Burke even went so far as to criticize the HRC for attacking Tyree.[35] Wade Davis echoed that in a piece he wrote for the Monday Morning Quarterback in which he described Tyree as being "on a journey when it comes to understanding the LGBT community. He is evolving." But Davis also cautioned that the former Giant wide receiver's "journey" is not complete. He vowed to "help him along his journey" and hopes that the outcome will be a "positive one."[36]

Well, here's hoping it's not a "positive one"—not because I think a man isn't entitled to change his opinion, but because a man shouldn't be compelled to change his opinion because of politically correct tyranny that denies alternative points of view. David Tyree was a brave and forceful voice for traditional marriage in the NFL, and it's not like there were many such voices willing to speak publicly. I have seen no evidence of Tyree recanting his beliefs. But let's not kid ourselves: activists like Burke and Davis aren't going to rush to Tyree's defense against fellow travelers like the HRC and wax eloquent about his philosophical evolution unless Tyree has said or done something to convince them that they should. It might appear that Tyree had to pay a ransom for his opinions, because once it was reported that he was on a "journey" and "evolving," the activists' criticism of him died down. Is that how it's going to be from now on? Will every traditional-marriage advocate, or every conservative, have to sit down with the politically correct tyrants and kiss the proverbial ring in order to get the crazies to shut up and leave him alone? It certainly seems that's the direction we're headed. I don't know if the Giants told Tyree to meet with Wade Davis or if he did it on his own initiative, but it sets the terrible precedent of giving activists who represent about 3 percent of the population near veto power over an NFL franchise's hiring a former player who happens to have exercised his First Amendment right to speak in favor of traditional marriage. Even when these activists lose, they win.

Alas, the practice of gay extortion is not confined to the HRC. Perhaps the most famous example of this comes from an NFL player. Chris Kluwe, a former punter for the Minnesota Vikings, supports gay marriage and has a history of loudly making his views known. He also happened to be an older and increasingly expensive player as the 2013 season approached. Just prior to the start of the season, the Vikings cut Kluwe, and no other NFL team signed him that year.

In 2014, with his career apparently over, Kluwe decided to give life to his bitterness toward the Vikings by writing a provocative tell-all for *Deadspin*. Kluwe could have chosen one of two roads when he penned his tale. One was the high road. The other was the one that he took. Here is the gist of his piece, "I Was an NFL Player Until I Was Fired by Two Cowards and a Bigot," as related by the *New York Daily News*:

> "It's my belief, based on everything that happened over the course of 2012, that I was fired by [special teams coach] Mike Priefer, a bigot who didn't agree with the cause I was working for, and two cowards, Leslie Frazier and [general manager] Rick Spielman, both of whom knew I was a good punter and would remain a good punter for the foreseeable future, as my numbers over my eight-year career had shown, but who lacked the fortitude to disagree with Mike Priefer on a touchy subject matter," Kluwe wrote in the 3,700-word piece, adding that he doesn't know for sure if his activism led to his dismissal from the team, "However I'm pretty confident it was."
>
> Priefer vehemently denied Kluwe's allegations in a statement given to Minnesota's KFAN sports radio. And in a separate statement released Thursday afternoon, the Vikings said they are taking Kluwe's claims seriously and "will thoroughly review this matter."[37]

Kluwe didn't leave the matter there, threatening to sue the Vikings for wrongful termination, claiming that his stance on gay marriage, not his performance, led to his being cut. This is interesting, since Kluwe, by his own admission, could not prove that his personal politics caused his release.

In fact, at the end of the *Deadspin* piece, Kluwe himself even went so far as to outline a couple of really, really good reasons for firing him, citing his "age" and his expensive "veteran minimum salary."[38] He might have added that the Vikings ranked twentieth in the NFL in punting average during Kluwe's last season with the team. That's certainly not good, and not something worth paying a ton of money for. But, of course, he left that part out.

The Vikings opened their own investigation into Kluwe's case, asking former chief justice of the Minnesota Supreme Court Eric Magnuson and former U.S. Department of Justice trial attorney Chris Madel "to complete an independent review of Kluwe's allegations" and "to thoroughly and comprehensively investigate three particular allegations by Kluwe and Kluwe's counsel," namely:

1. Special Teams Coordinator Mike Priefer made offensive and insensitive remarks in Kluwe's presence.
2. Representatives of the Vikings discouraged Kluwe from publicly supporting marriage equality and had knowledge of the Priefer comments prior to the *Deadspin* article publication on January 2, 2014.
3. Kluwe's activism for marriage equality was the reason for his release from the Vikings on May 6, 2013.[39]

The investigative team concluded that, basically, Chris Kluwe was full of garbage. They found evidence that Priefer had made *one* homophobic remark, but only after the coach became exasperated that Kluwe and his long snapper Cullen Loeffler weren't focusing on football. There was, on the other hand, *no* evidence that Vikings management knew about this remark. Moreover, according to the report, "The record supports the conclusion that players and management were concerned about the distraction that Kluwe's activism was creating, as opposed to the nature and content of his activism. The record does not support the contention that members of management and the coaching staff were focused on discouraging Kluwe based on the nature of his activism."[40]

According to the investigation:

> Kluwe himself stated that he never reported any of Priefer's alleged statements to management, Human Resources, or anyone else other than in discussions with [long snapper Cullen] Loeffler and [kicker Blair] Walsh [who issued a statement supporting Priefer's integrity and professionalism].... During his interview, investigators asked Kluwe why he did not bring Priefer's comments to the attention of others within the Vikings organization sooner. Kluwe explained that at the time, he did not know he was going to be released from the Vikings so he thought Priefer's remarks were "a momentary unpleasant thing" that would pass as they moved on to the next year.[41]

Translation: Chris Kluwe was so horrified by Priefer's alleged homophobic quip that he waited for the team to release him and then came up with this garbage story to look like a martyr.

Other findings from the commission make Kluwe look like an ass, almost literally. After news broke of the Jerry Sandusky child-abuse scandal at Penn State, Kluwe, according to a memorandum released by the Vikings and quoted in Pro Football Talk:

> …made fun of the Vikings' then Head Strength and Conditioning Coach Tom Kanavy, an alumnus of and former coach at Penn State University…. In his interview, Kanavy explained that Kluwe cut the seat out of his pants and then put them on to imitate a victim of the Penn State child-abuse scandal. According to Kanavy, Kluwe said that he was a "Penn State victim" and to "stay away" from him while his buttocks were exposed.
>
> Kluwe told investigators that he did not recall that behavior, but that "it's very possible" that he did it.
>
> "It didn't stick in my mind, but, you know, I—it is definitely—if people said they saw it, then yeah, I probably did it," Kluwe said.[42]

So, they want us to believe that the same guy who makes light of the rape of several young boys at the hands of a monster was mortally offended by a single homophobic remark made in frustration by a coach who though Kluwe wasn't focused on his job? Not buying it. Kluwe trashed what little credibility he had left when he took to Twitter after the release of the Vikings' investigative report and memorandum: "Oooh, shall we talk about the time two very well-known Vikings players were caught in a compromising situation with an underage girl?"[43] In a follow-up tweet, Kluwe said: "Bet you didn't hear about that one in the news. We can do this all day, Vikings. Special teams hears *everything*."[44]

Hmm, so to get this straight: Chris Kluwe, moral champion and defender of the LGBT realm, not only made fun of the rape of young boys, but apparently turned a blind eye and a deaf ear to the rape of a young girl?

Yet, despite the fact that Kluwe's charges were proved baloney and that he had exposed himself as a scumbag of the highest order, what did the Vikings do? They caved. To start, the Vikings suspended special teams coach Mike Priefer for three games. Then the team agreed to provide an undisclosed sum of money to five different LGBT charities, and to host a national conference on LGBT issues in the field of professional athletics, *and* to mandate sensitivity training four times a year for all Vikings employees. To top it all off, the Vikings donated an additional $100,000 to LGBT charities, over and above the undisclosed amount already given to the other five charities.[45]

Al Sharpton has nothing on this corporate shakedown. Facts no longer matter. Only image and fear matter. The Vikings, and really all sports organizations, now simply manage image, tempered solely by the fear of appearing insensitive, as defined by pressure groups and the liberal media.

The liberal sports media that tried to make heroes of Michael Sam, Jason Collins, and Chris Kluwe only showed how ridiculously partisan, lacking in any rational perspective, and off-topic they can be. Sports fans deserve better.

CHAPTER FIVE

TRASHING TEBOW

Watercooler talk at the office is awesome, because everyone gets together to talk about things that have nothing to do with work. But in radio it's different. Your watercooler talk is our meat and potatoes. And so it was that, as cut-down day loomed in the NFL and Tim Tebow prepared to learn his fate, I was standing in front of the studio's break-room microwave waiting for the beep and instead I heard a loud scream: "Yes!"

Turning around, I saw a coworker with a beaming grin on his face: "Tebow is out! Somebody *finally* got rid of that Jesus freak!"

"Oh, yeah?" I said. "I feel bad for him. I don't think the religious stuff really hurt anybody. He should be on a roster somewhere." He had, after all, led the Broncos to the playoffs in 2011–12 after a series of thrilling come-from-behind wins.

"Well, you know, man, he can be who he is; I'm not saying all that. I just don't like it when people wear that stuff on their sleeve."

"Well, where should he have worn it? Why should he keep it to himself if it's something he believes in?"

My work buddy, stunned to find someone not part of the liberal groupthink, backed out of the room, saying, "I feel you, dawg. I feel you…"

If I were more naïve, I'd be shocked that the sports media so hated such a well-meaning, harmless, good-works-doing kid as Tim Tebow.

But while sports journalists can tolerate an index finger raised to heaven after a touchdown or even a prayer circle after a game, they don't like players to talk about it and walk the Christian walk in public. Tebow is not just a Christian who "tebows" after touchdowns. He lives his faith in ways that, to lefty sports journalists, make him a threat to the totally secular sports world they are determined to create. (Sports journalists, in case you haven't noticed, are terrific at moral reversals.) So the fact that Tebow spends his summers helping at a family-run orphanage, building a children's hospital, and preaching the gospel is something sports commentators actually hold against him, particularly that last part.

In college, Tebow spent more time in prison than most college athletes—and that's saying something. But he wasn't making license plates, he was conducting a prison ministry. Tebow's parents are Baptist missionaries, and Tebow has taken up that role too. It is very hard for liberal, amoral sports reporters not to want to rebuke someone like that, especially when the player and the missionary are inseparable.

The whole Tebow package—tebowing after a touchdown, the "pro-life" Tebow Super Bowl commercial (where his mother talks about how Tebow "almost didn't make it into this world" and how she still worries about him—before he tackles her...about the most inoffensive pro-life message imaginable), and the mass popularity of Tebow as a Christian sports hero—scared the sports media. It wasn't merely that Tebow had religion, it was that he used his celebrity to evangelize. The liberal sports media viewed him as a monster, even though he was a monster they had helped create because he made good copy and was good for ratings.

With more than eighty colleges recruiting him out of high school, Tebow was the subject of a documentary in ESPN's *Faces of Sports* series. It showcased his incredible on-the-field exploits but also covered the family's strong Christian faith. The documentary showed Tebow's father, Bob, reading scripture and talking about how he had prayed for a son named Timothy whom he could raise to be a preacher. The piece went into, albeit briefly, how doctors told Pam, Tebow's mother, that she would die if she did not abort the future Tim, and how she defied their advice, literally risking her life for the benefit of her unborn child. It was an extremely well-done, powerful, and uplifting piece of journalism.

The sports media profiles continued through his college years, depicting Tebow's religion in a light that, if not flattering, was at least not overtly critical. As his fame grew at Florida and he established himself as one of the best college football players of his class, Tebow became more comfortable in front of the cameras, talking God and football to millions. By the time he arrived in the NFL, he was seen by many as what was once called a "muscular Christian," an evangelist who could take on a Mike linebacker in the open field.

However, once Tebow got into the pros, the lefty NFL media were quick to put "Saint Timmy" on notice that the mostly positive media coverage he had received in high school and college was over. In fact, Tim Tebow couldn't even get out of the NFL combine before the proverbial lions were released. As Gregg Rosenthal wrote on Pro Football Talk, "Quarterback Tim Tebow's habit of openly expressing his religious beliefs could potentially rub folks the wrong way, especially in a locker room of grown men who choose to keep their beliefs to themselves, who don't share his beliefs at all, and/or who only want to hear 'God bless' after they have sneezed."[1]

Gregg's strange line that "Tebow's habit of openly expressing his religious beliefs could potentially rub folks the wrong way, *especially in a locker room full of grown men* [emphasis added]" implied a deep disdain for Christianity, treating it as a fairy tale that Saint Timmy might still believe but that grown men don't. But put the typical liberal media contempt for Christianity aside for a minute and think about the double standard here. The same media that would later cheer the prospect of an openly gay player in an NFL locker room and didn't care if it rubbed anyone "the wrong way"—that in fact called such people "bigots"—thought it disruptive to have an openly Christian player like Tebow in a locker room. That's not just a double standard: that's crazy.

But that was just the opening salvo of Rosenthal's piece. The larger context came via a report from the NFL combine that before taking the Wonderlic test (the NFL IQ test administered to all players) Tim Tebow summoned the athletes together for a group prayer. "Per a league source," Rosenthal reported, one of the players said in response:

> "Shut the f–k up." Other players in the room then laughed.
>
> We're not passing judgment on this one; we're just passing along what we've heard. And it illustrates the type of challenges that could be faced by the team that drafts Tebow.[2]

After Rosenthal's story came out, Tebow contacted Pro Football Talk, denied that anything like this happened, and even named the players in the room and invited Rosenthal to call them.

Rosenthal's dire warning of how Tebow's religion could be a problem was based on a single highly suspect account of an occurrence at the combine, one very convenient for Rosenthal's piece. There was, however, no record of Tebow's religion being a problem with the Florida Gators, where he had been a team captain, or with his high school teammates. Like so much of leftist sports journalism, Rosenthal's story was centered on opinion, his own and that of those who agreed with him, rather than facts.

It also illustrates the complete disconnect between the sports media and the athletes they cover. News flash: NFL players are overwhelmingly Christian, as is the country at large. Rosenthal's assertion that it would be problematic to add an evangelical Christian player to a locker room full of Christian players, nominal or not, is beyond absurd.

One could say that Rosenthal failed to do his due diligence as a reporter. But equally important is the *way* this story was reported. If we lived in a sane world, the villain of the piece would be the alleged hurler of the F-bomb, not the fellow praying for his success. What if, at the NFL combine, a player yelled out at Michael Sam as he was being interviewed, "Shut the f–k up"? Do you think the sports media would have passed this along as one of the dangers of drafting Michael Sam? Or do you think they would have named and shamed the F-bomb shouter?

Rosenthal claimed not to be "passing judgment on this one"[3]— as if there's some kind of gray area between Christianity and "shut the f–k up"—but as a reporter, shouldn't he have tried to find out who allegedly said it, you know, to confirm the story? Rosenthal claimed he would "keep digging"[4] on the story after Tebow said it didn't happen. Yet despite all the "digging," no one identified the alleged culprit. Seems odd, right? After all, when the sports media want to expose someone, they do it. We all remember ESPN's Darren Rovell and shady hotel-room footage of Johnny Manziel signing football helmets, telling camera operators, "You never did a signing with me."[5] We remember the near-Orwellian lip-reading tactics used on Kobe Bryant when he called NBA referee Bennie Adams a "f—ing faggot,"[6] which of course sparked a massive gay-outreach program by the NBA. But the sports media seemed content to the let the combine story drop.

There's another explanation as to why the sports media never produced Tim Tebow's F-bomb hurler, and that's because he never existed in the first place. Pro Football Talk's promises to "keep digging," coupled with Tebow's stringent denial, smack of a story whose basis in fact was flimsy at best. That in itself could have been a story, but if you think the liberal sports media are interested in journalistic standards, you obviously haven't been paying attention.

Pro Football Talk's "reporting" was just the tip of the iceberg for the USS Tebow. When he landed on the Denver Broncos, serving as Kyle Orton's backup, he was consistently peppered with questions about what he thought his prospects were of one day landing the starting job. Sometimes the questions were less flattering, sounding more like statements of how he didn't have what it took to be a consistent starter in the NFL, to which he once replied, "Others who say I won't make it are wrong. They don't know what I'm capable of and what's inside me. My family and my friends have been bothered by what's gone on, and I tell them to pay no attention to it. I'm relying as always on my faith."[7]

Pretty innocuous statement there, right? I mean, pro athletes frequently speak of how they have faith in themselves and faith in God. But CBS Sports' Gregg Doyel heard Tebow's words and hastily penned a column making some of the most ludicrous claims ever made from a harmless quote. "Unbelievable," Doyel cried in the headline. "Tebow Believes Faith Equates to Starting in NFL."[8] Doyel inserted all the semi-mandatory "I'm not against religion" disclaimers and the obligatory "I go to church myself" qualifier at the beginning of the piece, then without skipping a beat went about demonstrating no understanding of religious faith whatsoever as he summed up Tebow's quote thus: "He'll make it in this league—for the Bible tells him so."[9]

"Tebow is rightfully confident," Doyel went on. "But his confidence isn't only in himself. It's in his God. Tebow has basically said, and I'm paraphrasing here, 'I'll be a starter in this league because God loves me that much.'"[10] Doyel wrote, also in his own words, that Tebow's faith seems to be that he "will be rewarded with a starting job in the NFL."[11]

Holy overanalysis, Batman! First of all, it really would have been swell if Doyel had actually . . . you know . . . *asked Tebow* what he meant by saying he was "relying on faith." Apparently that didn't happen. Perhaps if he had asked, Tebow would have said that "relying on faith" doesn't mean everything works out the way you want it to; it's a belief that *no matter what comes*, you'll be okay, because it's all part of God's plan. I'm pretty sure I read that somewhere.

All of Doyel's ignorance and spin and lack of due diligence I could forgive, but there's no forgiving what Doyel said in his last paragraph:

Tebow has been a great billboard for Christianity—just as Muhammad Ali has been a great billboard for Islam, and Sandy Koufax a great billboard for Judaism—but that doesn't mean he will be rewarded with a starting job in the NFL. Maybe deep inside his heart Tebow knows that, but from the outside it doesn't look that way. From the outside it looks like Tebow equates his love for God in heaven with tangible rewards here on earth. And that's more than wrong. It's blasphemy.[12]

Really? So now we have sports commentators defining *blasphemy* for us, and typically they define it in a self-serving, double-standard way. Somehow it passes liberal sports reporters by that part of faith is *gratitude* for the gifts God has given you. When a player scores a touchdown and raises his finger skyward, he's not saying, "God thinks I'm great," but rather, "Thanks, God, for giving me the talent to do this." But even supposing for a second that Doyel is right, that Tim Tebow "equates his love for God in heaven with tangible rewards here on earth," how many athletes, and Christians at large for that matter, thank God for "His blessings" and think those blessings come, at least in part, from their love of God? When Florida State's Jameis Winston praised God after winning the BCS National Championship game, was he saying that his faith in God had helped deliver him the title? Maybe—again, at least in part. Did Kurt Warner equate religion with success when on the podium with Terry Bradshaw after winning the 2009 NFC Championship game he said, "There's one reason that I'm standing up on this stage today, and that's because of my Lord up above.... I've got to say thanks to Jesus!"?[13] Yet I don't recall anyone writing a column calling Winston or Warner blasphemous because they credited their success on the football field to God.

But that's precisely what Gregg Doyel did to Tim Tebow because Tebow is more overtly a missionary for his faith and therefore, if you're part of the liberal sports media, a greater threat.

Especially disappointing about the Tebow saga is that when fellow Christian athletes had the chance to get Tebow's back and help defend their shared faith, they instead let him be fed to the lions. No one was more disappointing in this regard than Kurt Warner. Something funny happened to Kurt after he stopped playing and took a commentary spot for the NFL Network. When asked about Tebow and his brand of expressive faith, Warner told the *Washington Post* that Tebow should "put down the boldness in regards to the words, and keep living the way you're living."[14] I love Kurt Warner, but that's a complete cop-out. Did Kurt Warner "put down the boldness" when he shouted, "I've got to say thanks to Jesus!" to Terry Bradshaw? In fact, you could make the argument that Kurt Warner was Tebow before Tebow, frequently making his faith a public part of his life.

But that was when Warner was a player in the league. Look at the transformation in Warner from player to broadcaster, from Mr. Thank-You-Jesus to Mr. Tone-It-Down Guy. Why? Because he knew, or was flat out told, that kind of talk would not be tolerated in the sports media. If Kurt Warner were gay, and Tim Tebow had been the first active, openly gay athlete in a major American sport, there's no way Kurt Warner would have felt compelled to tell Tebow to tone anything down. On the contrary, he would have demanded a one-hour exclusive interview, complete with footage of Tebow snogging his boyfriend, because homosexuality is embraced by the leftist American sports media. Christianity is not.

I remember one day hearing an outbreak of laughter and choruses of "Oh yeah!" coming from the newsroom. Running at my age and girth from the copier to the newsroom takes a while, but the mood was still jubilant when I arrived. It didn't take me long to see why. Stephen Tulloch of the Detroit Lions had sacked Tebow and then mocked the famous on-the-field prayer gesture of the quarterback. One of our board-ops was beside himself with joy: "Take that, motherfucker!"

It was quite a scene. And this was a newsroom in Houston, Texas, where *nobody* gave a rip about the Broncos *or the Lions*, and yet they were thrilled, because the quarterback who committed the "crime" of prayer had gotten his. Nor did any condemnation or anger come from any of the media for what Tulloch had done. I'm not saying Tulloch is anti-Christian; I don't know what's in his heart. For all I know, he was only trying to mock the young celebrity player he had just sacked (I feel pretty strongly that he has that in his heart). But regardless of his intent, here was an NFL player mocking the deeply held religious faith of a fellow player on the field of play. Yet it was met with deafening silence by the overwhelming majority of the sports media—well, except when they were shouting, "Take that, motherfucker!"

But as Todd Starnes of Fox News wrote shortly after this happened, "Imagine for just a moment if Tebow had been a Muslim. Imagine Tulloch sacking the quarterback and then pulling out a prayer rug and offering a mocking prayer toward Mecca. Imagine that."[15] Imagine indeed. Stephen Tulloch probably would have been suspended, and I don't just mean from football. I mean suspended in mid-air with a pack of press hyenas nipping at his dangling feet. *Sports Illustrated* might even have run a cover with Stephen Tulloch's face on it asking if Tulloch was too hateful for the NFL, the same way the magazine once asked if Chuck Cecil was too violent for the NFL.

President Obama might have weighed in. Actually, I guarantee President Obama would have weighed in. Because if a faith *other than*

Christianity had been mocked, then the media would have seen fit to respond. But Christianity? Meh. No biggie. In fact, this point was made by none other than KISS front man Gene Simmons, who absolutely nailed the media for their hypocrisy on Tebow:

> He's got a religious passion, as well he should, we're in America. He's proud to be a Christian, what's wrong with that? And yet, with sports media and pop culture media, they make fun of his religion. Really? In America? If he was wearing a burqa, they wouldn't dare say anything.
>
> But if you're a Christian, you get to be picked on? What the hell?[16]

It's a scary day when a guy best known for leather body suits and an impressive tongue length makes more sense than the American sports media. But that's precisely what's happened here. And yes, it's true that only Muslim *women* wear burqas. But change that to a keffiyeh or a taj, both traditional headgear worn by Muslim men, and his point is still well made. The sports media are just as terrified of provoking Muslim outrage as the mainstream media are, and they would in no way be telling Tebow to "tone it down" if he prayed on a carpet instead of bended knee.

There's also—and many people disagree with me about this (which must mean that I'm right), but I'm going to say it anyway—a very strong racial component to the Tebow coverage. Many proud and openly Christian athletes have come through the NFL over the years, but up until recently the most high profile of these have been black. Reggie White, for one, was an *ordained minister* (hence his nickname, the Minister of Defense). Yet Reggie White did not receive the same level of hatred as Tim Tebow, though he was outspoken about his faith, was vocal in the community, and preached at his church every single weekend.

Sure, people got upset in 1998 when he told the Wisconsin state legislature he thought marriage should be between a man and a woman. But that was late into his career, and he had said things before that didn't garner the same media backlash. Reggie White used to spend hours and hours every day reading and memorizing the Bible. He's also the same player who once told an opposing offensive lineman that "Jesus was coming" right before he fired out of his stance and planted the aforementioned tackle on his backside.

Could you imagine if Tebow had shouted, "Jesus is coming!" before running a zone read or a quarterback sneak? Bob Costas would have had a stroke. White is also the one famous for singing a stirring rendition of "Amazing Grace" that every football fan over the age of thirty has no doubt seen at least eleventy times. Point being, Reggie White's faith was every bit as deeply held as Tebow's. White was also a bona fide first-ballot Hall of Famer and one of *the* most dominant defensive players in NFL history. You would think his faith would be as scrutinized as Tebow's by an unfriendly media, but it wasn't.

Former NFL coach Tony Dungy, the first black head coach to win the Super Bowl, was appointed to serve on former president George W. Bush's Council on Service and Civic Participation, and then invited to join President Obama's Advisory Council on Faith-Based and Neighborhood Partnerships (which he declined). Clearly he was known for his faith. In fact, at Super Bowl XLI, when Dungy's Colts faced Lovie Smith's Bears, Dungy had the nerve to ruin CBS's pre– and post–Super Bowl meme of talking up the first Super Bowl between two black head coaches by focusing instead on what he thought was the more significant trait he and Lovie Smith shared.

"This is a great time for both of us," Dungy said. "I'm so happy Lovie got to the Super Bowl because he does things the right way. He's gotten there with a lot of class…no intimidation, just helping his guys play the best they can. That's the way I try to do it and I think it's great we've been able to show the world that not only can African-American coaches do it, *but Christian coaches* [emphasis added] can do it in a way that, you know, we can still win."[17]

After the game, the *New York Times* quickly moved in to course-correct Dungy and make sure you didn't get the wrong idea that God was the real story here:

> In the midst of the rain and confetti falling on Dolphin Stadium on Sunday night, two men embraced near mid-field and held on tight.
>
> They were linked by football and friendship, faith and success. *But Tony Dungy and Lovie Smith also shared a broader distinction: being the first African-Americans to coach a team to the Super Bowl* [emphasis added].[18]

So being black is the "broader distinction," huh? That's funny, because Tony Dungy seemed to go out of his way to make it clear that he thought it was the other way around. In Dungy's own words: "I tell you what, I'm proud to be representing African-American coaches, to be the first African-American coach to win this. It means an awful lot to our country. But again, *more than anything*, I said it before, Lovie Smith and I, not only the first two African-Americans, *but Christian coaches showing you can win doing it the Lord's way. We're more proud of that* [emphasis added]."[19]

Never let the facts get in the way of a good story.

But what's interesting too is how Reggie White's and Tony Dungy's Christian faith and controversial opinions never caused a media storm the way Tebow's faith did. Yes, Dungy took some media flack for saying that he wouldn't have drafted Michael Sam, but it was mild-mannered stuff compared with what Tebow has endured. No sports radio host has ever likened Dungy's family to Nazis.

Of course, nothing stirred the ire of the liberal sports media more than the perfectly harmless Focus on the Family Super Bowl ad that Tebow and his mother Pam appeared in during the 2010 Super Bowl. For all the hype that commercial received, you would have thought the Tebows planned to slaughter the fatted calf right there on national television. Instead, it turned out to be a nice, even slightly goofy, commercial about the love a mother can have for her child (even if unborn) and what can become of her child if given a chance at life (like winning the Heisman Trophy). But even this innocuous thirty-second ode to life was too much to escape the scorn of CBS's Gregg Doyel: "If you're a sports fan, and I am, that's the holiest day of the year. It's not a day to discuss abortion. For it, against it, I don't care what you are. On Super Sunday, I don't care what I am. Feb. 7 is simply not the day to have that discussion."[20]

Of course, abortion was not even mentioned in the ad. In fact, if you were like most Super Bowl viewers—munching chips, drinking a beer, talking with friends—the only thing you probably noticed was Tebow tackling his mom. This wasn't an ad you had to shield the kids from. It wasn't an ad that was loud and brash and trying to be more important than the game. It was an innocent thirty-second football-themed spot about a mother's love for her son. How flipping controversial is that?

The CBS/AP story, which quoted Doyel, didn't bother to get any quotations from sportswriters who *were not* offended by the Tebow ad, but maybe that's because the other sportswriters they called were cowering under their desks in the fetal position, as they usually do when abortion comes up, and were "unavailable for comment." It is interesting, however, that Doyel uses the word "holiest" to describe a sporting event. He's being deliberately provocative in calling a football game "holy"—and life, family, and faith something less than that (the ad's tagline was "Celebrate family, celebrate life"). For abortion and against abortion, he says, "I don't care what you are...I don't care what I am. Feb. 7 is simply not the day to have that discussion." So life and death, right and wrong cease to matter when the NFL decides to have a championship game?

But, in all honesty, Tebow had been marked for destruction long before his Super Bowl ad came out. The ad merely gave the sports media another opportunity to vent against Tebow and everything he stands for, and there are few issues that provide a starker dividing line than "life." The liberal sports media are opposed to anything that restricts "freedom" below the waist. So Tebow's "celebrating family, celebrating life" in a thirty-second spot was far more offensive to them than one of those titillating GoDaddy ads that provide awkward moments for family viewing. Go figure.

Over the years, though, there have been a few brave voices in the sports media who have "called out their own" on the Tim Tebow saga. On Showtime's *Inside the NFL*, host James Brown and former Bengals wide receiver Cris Collinsworth discussed the treatment of Tebow, and Collinsworth didn't hold back: "It's unbelievable, though, J. B., that one of the best kids—just pure kids that's ever come into the NFL—is hated because of his faith, because of his mission work, because of the fact that he wears it on his sleeve, because of the fact that he lives his life that he talks about."[21]

Former 49ers offensive lineman, three-time Super Bowl champ, and current CBS sports analyst Randy Cross was equally direct on the subject: "People, especially the media, root against him because of what he stands for.... My personal belief is there are people in the media, people in the stands, who are predisposed to see a guy like that fail.... Just because he's so public about the way he feels."[22]

James Brown, in his conversation with Collinsworth on *Inside the NFL*, opined, "There's a number of guys who come into the league with a big marquee, fat paychecks, a lot of attention, and folks don't seem to hate them with the same intensity that they hate Tim Tebow." Collinsworth commented: "I couldn't agree with you more. And it's kind of a sad commentary, that, you know, if someone is out carousing every night, the Joe Namath thing, or whatever, they're American heroes, and Tim Tebow, who's working in missions in Asia somewhere, is a guy that we're going to vilify."[23] And that really sums it up, doesn't it?

Given all the criminal news on the sports pages, the NFL should be starving for some wholesome inspiration, and Tim Tebow should have been held up as a role model rather than vilified for—well, for his goodness, for crying out loud.

A kid growing up in the 1960s had to wait until he was in his thirties before he found out that Mickey Mantle was a drunk. A kid growing up in the 1920s had to wait until he was in his fifties before he learned Babe Ruth was a violent drinker, and a womanizer to boot. Thanks to twenty-four-hour cable sports television, radio, and print, our kids find out the dirty laundry on their heroes in real time. In such a polluted landscape, a good guy like Tim Tebow was an uncontaminated wellspring of hope for a lot of people—a reminder that faith, hard work, and determination, values that coaches used to instill in their players, sometimes met their reward. Remember when we used to think that sports taught character? Tebow was a throwback to that. But the sports media are more comfortable with players who "make it rain" at the strip bars downtown.

And if you didn't like Tebow's stance on abortion, fine; ignore it the same way I ignore the seven children, as of this writing, that Adrian Peterson has fathered out of wedlock when I cheer his brilliance on the football field. Ignore Tebow's tebowing the same way Eagles fans ignored Michael Vick's dog-torturing and mutilation when they cheered for him. People in Denver appeared to have no problem ignoring whatever they didn't like about "Saint Timmy" when he became the come-from-behind sensation who led his team to the playoffs. It was the members of the sports media who had the problem.

A lot of people have become quite comfortable over the years cheering for their favorite athletes, even if they sometimes have to hold their noses when they do it. The point is that whatever the source of Tebow's goodness, what is indisputable is that he was good for the sports world, and he had a whole lot more in common with the average everyday fan than the multimillion-dollar players who live like gangsters. But that wasn't good enough for the sports media. No, they chewed him up and spat him out, because their values and your values are not the same.

CHAPTER SIX

CONCUSSED AND CONFUSED

witter is truly an awesome thing. Right next to ketchup, the internet, the wheel, fire, and the Red Zone Channel, it is a solid member in good standing among the top ten greatest inventions of all time. Twitter is great for many reasons, but chiefly because it's nothing but raw, unfiltered opinion. People's honesty comes through in a way that it doesn't in more traditional formats. And it was while I was consuming this veritable cornucopia of unfiltered human thought one morning that I came across *USA Today* college football writer Dan Wolken tweeting from the American Football Coaches Association convention in January 2014. The tweets seemed harmless enough at first: quotations from speakers discussing concussions in football and some of the misconceptions that have been formed. Then Wolken tweeted: "This is a total pep rally for football."[1]

Okay, so what did Wolken expect at a coaches association meeting? A condemnation of football? Wolken's *pièce de résistance* wasn't long in coming: "Is football safety going to be like the climate change debate? Don't like the research? Find a new researcher."[2]

Ta da! There you have it. Not only are all the coaches at the AFCA "pep rallying" for football, they've now assumed the role of global-warming/climate-change deniers! You see, in the minds of the leftist American sports media, football is "the new smoking" and is certain to bring about the next global apocalypse, largely because they're convinced that the link between playing football and long-term debilitating brain damage is "settled science." Apparently you'd be better off taking a pull on a Marlboro Red than putting on pads and cleats, and "science" has already settled the issue.

Now, this book is about the sports media, not about scientists, so I'm not going to get all *Myth Busters* on you here. But there are plenty of areas in life where science is far from "settled"—everything from diet advice, which changes daily, to the origin of the world (Big Bang or something else?), up to and including, as it turns out, global warming, where, for instance, scientists like Patrick Moore (an ecologist and early leader of Greenpeace), Patrick Michaels (a climatologist), and MIT professor of atmospheric science Richard Lindzen all have views starkly at odds with those of non-scientist and global-warming alarmist Al Gore. Didn't know that? Most sports reporters don't either.

And yes, not all scientists agree that football is wiping out the male population of the United States. Yet in a twist of journalistic masochism on a scale heretofore unseen, the leftist American sports media have decided to swallow the football-is-the-new-smoking meme hook, line, and sinker. They've essentially joined the crusade against the pigskin, despite the fact that the American sports media need football for their survival.

In 2013, according to SportsMediaWatch.com, the top twenty-six most-watched television sporting events were NFL games. Sixteen of those twenty-six were in the regular season, not playoff or championship games.[3] The NBA would have had to showcase LeBron wrestling a live cougar to get those kinds of ratings for a regular season game. In fact, none of the association's post-season games did well enough to crack the top twenty-six. Ditto for baseball, whose World Series ratings are slugging it out with the lowly NHL. Taking it a step further, forty-six of the top fifty most-watched television sporting events in 2013 were NFL games. ESPN is paying the NFL $15.2 billion through 2021.[4] That's $1.9 billion a year, and that's just for *Monday Night Football*. That's just for the rights to broadcast seventeen regular season games a year.

And then there's the money that Fox, CBS, and NBC pay the league to broadcast regular season games, playoff games, and the Super Bowl. My point here is not to further massage the already well-massaged ego of the National Football League. My point is that in the American sports world, the NFL is king and no one else is even close. In fact, you could argue that American sports media wouldn't even exist in their current position of power if it weren't for the NFL.

Yet, more than anything else, more than journalistic ethics (which entails getting both sides of a story), more than economic self-interest, more than serving the interests of its audience, the sports media are driven, lemming like, by political correctness, and political correctness dictates that football is bad for us. Even President Obama has weighed in, saying he wouldn't let his son, if he had one, play football. So the sports media are actually trying to kill their golden goose.

The only thing that could bring the NFL down, the thing that represents a clear and present danger to the future of the sport, is lawsuits. Specifically, concussion-related class-action lawsuits that could cost the league billions and result in Commissioner Roger Goodell's and other NFL leaders' being grilled on Capitol Hill and threatened with government oversight.

And yet, though they eventually pulled out of the production, who do you think assisted PBS in putting together its *Frontline* documentary *League of Denial*,[5] which charged that the NFL willfully and knowingly covered up the fact that players' brains were being turned to mush while Roger Goodell and his fat-cat owner buddies raked in the billions? Yes, that would be ESPN.

Now, I'm not saying that football is a completely safe sport. Of course it's not. Anyone who believes that probably already suffers from some kind of brain damage. What I am saying is that to liberals in the sports media, the link between the NFL and concussions is "settled" by their ideology rather than science. Their real concern is social justice and making those fat-cat owners pay reparations to the downtrodden—overwhelmingly minority—players who serve them. Don't believe me? In January 2014, on a Sunday right before the NFL's divisional round playoff games, ESPN ran a promo for a segment featuring Malcolm Gladwell. For those of you who don't know, Malcolm Gladwell is the guy who penned *Outliers*, which chronicled the lives and habits of successful people, and *Tipping Point*, which sought to explain mysterious sociological changes that mark everyday life. He's also the guy who said that football is no different from dogfighting:

> In what way is dog fighting any different from football on
> a certain level, right? I mean you take a young, vulnerable

dog who was made vulnerable because of his allegiance to the owner and you ask him to engage in serious sustained physical combat with another dog under the control of another owner, right?

Well, what's football? We take young boys, essentially, and we have them repeatedly, over the course of the season, smash each other in the head, with known neurological consequences.

And why do they do that? Out of an allegiance to their owners and their coaches and a feeling they're participating in some grand American spectacle.[6]

Still think I went too far when I said football and concussions fit in the liberal worldview? Does it sound like Gladwell is making a scientific argument here, or a political one? This argument is dripping with political and racial innuendo. If the science is so self-explanatory, then why resort to crass dogfighting analogies? Answer: Because this is the racial and class-warfare lens through which Gladwell and the sports media see the world. Now, to be clear, "young boys" are not forced to play football the way dogs are forced to fight each other. Dogs are not given a choice to fight; they have to and are almost certainly killed if they don't. Nobody is "forced" to play football. If the players decide they don't want to play anymore, they are not killed for it. In fact, on occasion they leave while costing their "owners" huge sums, as running back Ricky Williams did to then–Dolphins owner Wayne Huizenga when he decided he'd rather study massage therapy in India than continue to play football. Even college players are permitted to transfer from school to school.

Also, unlike dogs in dogfights, football players do not play until the other guy dies. As bad as the Jaguars are, nobody's going to let the Broncos kill them (though I understand that may disappoint many Jaguars fans). Nor do players play the game out of an "allegiance" to the owner. Many NFL players don't even know who the owner is. They play out of an allegiance to a game they love and for the grand American paycheck they receive for playing it. That paycheck is as close as many of them ever get to the owner. Even in college, the kids play for the scholarships and a chance to showcase their talents to the NFL scouts who will be evaluating them, not out of some ridiculous notion of "allegiance" to schools that wouldn't have given these players a second look were it not for their sub-4.5 forties.

But all that aside, don't you think it odd that on its NFL divisional playoff morning show, ESPN chose to showcase a guy who likens football to the lowest form of animal cruelty? If you were producing a show on how to prepare Thanksgiving turkey, would you invite a PETA activist to host the pre-show? Such a thing flies in the face of any kind of reason or common sense. But apparently in the corridors of power at Bristol, Connecticut (ESPN headquarters), nothing is thought to be amiss at having a football "denier" on the pregame show. Why? Because he thinks like they do.

Nor was Gladwell's dogfighting tirade the only negative thing he has said about our nation's favorite game. According to *Forbes* magazine:

> Gladwell mentioned the case of University of Pennsylvania lineman Owen Thomas, who committed suicide in 2010. An autopsy showed early stages of CTE (Chronic Traumatic Encephalopathy) in Thomas' brain—just as it was found in the brains of Dave Duerson and Junior Seau, professional players who also ended their lives in suicide. CTE is linked to depression and impulse control disorder,

so it is probable—though not certain—that it contributed to Thomas' death, since he had no documented history of depression.[7]

Now, I'm not a scientist, but then again, neither is Malcolm Gladwell. However, a researcher at *Harvard Medical School* named Grant Iverson is, and he studied the claim that NFL players are at increased risk of suicide and published his findings in the *British Journal of Sports Medicine*. As summarized by Daniel Flynn, author of the great book *The War on Football* (a must read if you want the truth on concussions and football):

> "Former NFL players were less likely to die by suicide than men in the general population," the doctor working in Harvard Medical School's Department of Physical Medicine and Rehabilitation notes of a comprehensive 2012 study of NFL veterans by the National Institute for Occupational Safety and Health (NIOSH). "There were only nine reported case[s] of suicide between 1960 and 2007. Therefore, according to the only published epidemiological data until now, NFL players are at decreased risk, not increased risk, for completed suicide relative to the general population."[8]

Moreover, not only are former NFL players less likely to commit suicide than people in the general population, it's not even clear to Dr. Iverson that concussions and/or CTE are even the causes of the few suicides that occur. Again, Flynn explains it:

> For instance, Iverson notes that suicide caused the deaths of just three of the thirty-three NFL players examined in a

recent journal article authored by researchers affiliated with Boston University's Center for the Study of Traumatic Encephalopathy. Among the non-NFL brains examined, the BU group reported ten suicides among the 53 decedents, with the majority of those suicide cases not demonstrating any signs of CTE. Of the minority of brains in which researchers did discover CTE among that group of ten non-NFL suicide cases, three exhibited just stage 1 or 2 CTE. In other words, most of the CTE cases didn't kill themselves, most of the suicide cases didn't have the disease, and most of the few who did exhibited a less advanced form of it.[9]

Or, put differently, the few former NFL players who choose to take their own lives likely do it for the same reasons that non-NFL players do it: They're miserable. They've made mistakes. They've lost their families, their money, whatever the case may be. As Flynn notes in an article on Breitbart.com, most of these high-profile NFL suicides had non-football-related mitigating factors:

> Bears defensive back Dave Duerson experienced home foreclosure, bankruptcy, and the failure of a marriage. Broncos offensive lineman Mike Current faced thirty years in prison for allegedly molesting three children. Chargers linebacker Junior Seau drank five or six nights a week, gambled excessively, relied on various prescription drugs to sleep, and faced the imminent loss of his San Diego steakhouse.[10]

Dr. Iverson even attempted to give alternative explanations for why NFL players might be committing suicide. As noted by Flynn:

"Iverson cites a study of Swedish athletes that showed a link between past steroid use and suicide among power lifters, wrestlers, and other competitors. Might these same factors induce some NFL players to experience depression and commit suicide?"[11]

Now, in a world with an unbiased, non-leftist-agenda-driven media, this information would be cause for serious pause. Even doubt. After all, any journalist honestly concerned with truth would look at the findings of a Harvard researcher like Dr. Iverson, coupled with the mitigating factors in all of these suicides, and think, "Hmmm. Maybe we should sit this play out and wait for the scientists to make up their minds before we jump to any conclusions." But not in the world we live in. No, in our world, any facts that differ from the sports media's talking points only convince the sports media that they need to talk more loudly to make sure nobody ever hears the "deniers." For example, Sally Jenkins, sports columnist for the *Washington Post*, wasted no time lashing out at the NFL with unsubstantiated data. While making her case that, during labor negotiations, NFL players will get hurt no matter the outcome, Jenkins said, "The suicide rate among ex-NFL players is six times the national average, according to GamesOver.org, a Web site dedicated to helping former players adjust to retirement."[12] Now, we can give Sally a break here, because the NIOSH findings were a few months away from being published—even though she could have proved that number wrong by doing her own, you know, job of investigating the claim before she printed it.

But what's Frank Bruni's excuse? In a *New York Times* article released months after the NIOSH findings were published, he made the same exact claim that Jenkins did, saying, "The suicide rate for men who have played in the N.F.L. is nearly six times the national average."[13] The NIOSH report also did not sway the hysterical bleating of Don Banks over at *Sports Illustrated*'s Monday Morning

Quarterback. In an article titled "What Price Football?," he chastised those who complain about NFL rule changes put in place for "safety," saying such critics should "worry less about new rules 'ruining' the game and more about the lives that have been ruined by the game, thanks to the effects of dementia, depression and suicides related to brain trauma. What we know about those issues today might wind up being just the tip of that scary iceberg."[14]

What's important to note here is that this article was written in October 2013, more than a full calendar year after the release of the NIOSH report, when it was apparent to anyone actually paying attention (so not necessarily sports reporters) that the suicide rate for NFL players was well below, not well above, the national average. What we knew was that there was no definitive link between football-incurred brain damage and suicide. And CTE was, at most, one of many factors causing suicides. But what we knew at the time and what Don Banks wrote are two entirely different things, because Banks didn't write that article as a journalist, he wrote it as a propagandist, desperate to keep an anti-football media agenda alive long after the facts started to take it apart. Ditto Frank Bruni. Which begs an interesting question: If covering football is your job, but you view football as a life-destroying, soul-sucking contagion, then why would you continue doing it? Why would you continue to sit there, day in and day out, producing articles for something called the Monday Morning Quarterback if all you thought the NFL was doing was producing future invalids, vegetables, and suicide cases?

I think most people would walk away from that. I think most people would find some other area to ply their trade, as opposed to covering a beat of death and disability from the NFL. But they don't. In fact, I'm unaware of any journalist who has laid down his pen, or dropped his microphone, and walked away in disgust over the "blood sport" spectacle he's being forced to comment on, and there are reasons for that. Yes, many of these commentators have made themselves a lot of money covering sports, which of course adds another level of hypocrisy to their whining about the league most directly responsible for their job security and affluence. But it goes deeper than that, much deeper. The real reason they're not walking away is because they have resolved to change the game from within, not because they're interested in "saving" NFL players. They're doing it to save you from yourself.

Bob Ryan of the *Boston Globe* let that proverbial cat out of the bag in his article titled "Football a Game of Inherent Conflict."[15] Who is Bob Ryan? Bob Ryan is the elder statesman of the sports media, not just in Boston, but nationally as well. That's not to say he's old and washed up—I've interviewed Bob many times, and he's as smart as anybody, if not smarter. He's also as respected as anybody, which means when he talks people listen, and normally he's not just speaking for himself. Bob Ryan is the Walter Cronkite of the sports media in a lot of ways: he is their voice and their soul. In his article, Ryan laid out the Left's "guilt pangs" at covering a sport that he refers to as "almost barbaric," and also how the sport may be stopped and done away with altogether. Referring to players and coaches, he writes: "Football has an enormous appeal to many people who are borderline psychopaths in a manner that no other sport—and this includes the very virile sport of hockey—does not."[16]

What's funny about this is that Bob Ryan works at ESPN in Bristol, Connecticut, which employs dozens of former NFL players and coaches, none of whom he'd probably want to call a borderline psychopath, at least not face-to-face. His point is that because football is so violent, it draws in those of "questionable moral character and mental make-up." It's not a game that is suitable for "normal" people. He goes on:

The simple truth is that football can never be made safe. Even if the essential "kill" mentality were changed, football can never be made safe. And it has never been more dangerous than it is now, thanks to a combination of there being larger, quicker, more lethal people delivering the blows and the lingering mentality brought to the game by coaches and players who cannot or will not change.[17]

So, even with all of our scientists and all of our technology, our efforts to protect the "psychopaths" from damaging their precious brains will come to naught, because it's impossible for the game to be made safe. Which, of course, leaves us with the question: Whatever are we to do about this "almost barbaric" scourge that is ruining so many lives? Bob Ryan provides the answer:

The mothers of America could shut down football today.

I'm not saying they're going to, but they could. The mothers of America could band together and say, "Uh-uh, no way. My boy's not playing football. And that's all there is to it."....

I come to you as an enabler, and I suspect there are many more out there like me. We are essentially troubled by the casual acceptance our society has of a sport that really and truly maims people. That football is America's current sport of choice reflects poorly on us as a people. But we enablers also have lived with this sport as long as we can remember and we understand it and appreciate its history. We enjoy a good game. And we know nothing we say or do will have an effect on the product. I'm going to guess that Super Bowl XLVIII will take place on Feb. 2,

2014. But Super Bowl LXXIV? Mothers of America, it's up to you.[18]

And there you have it. Here is the dean of the American sports media not only empowering the "mothers of America" by reminding them of the power they hold in not allowing their sons to play football, but essentially pleading with them to shut down football once and for all. He's saying, basically, "Hey, I can't stop this thing. I can't derail this crazy train. But you can! So unless you want your kids to spend the rest of their lives as vegetables, you better pull them from Pop Warner and get them going on something else. Or you'll have no one to blame except yourself." And you know what? It's working. According to statistics provided by Pop Warner football to ESPN's *Outside the Lines*:

> Pop Warner lost 23,612 players, thought to be the largest two-year decline since the organization began keeping statistics decades ago. Consistent annual growth led to a record 248,899 players participating in Pop Warner in 2010; that figure fell to 225,287 by the 2012 season. Pop Warner officials said they believe several factors played a role in the decline, including the trend of youngsters focusing on one sport. But the organization's chief medical officer, Dr. Julian Bailes, cited concerns about head injuries as "the No. 1 cause."[19]

Clearly the "mothers of America" are listening and have heard Bob Ryan's clarion call, which undercuts his very point that he and the liberal sports media are powerless to derail the NFL Express. Where, after all, did the 23,612 "mothers of America" who pulled their boys out of Pop Warner between 2010 and 2012 get their information? Where did they hear that concussions and CTE were prime factors in brain damage, suicide, twerking, global warming, and the shooting of J. R.? They heard it from Bob Ryan and his ilk, though they conveniently never heard the mounting evidence that completely contradicted these claims, showing that NFL suicides were lower than the national average and that CTE alone did not conclusively cause any of said suicides. That bit of deafening silence was also brought to you by Bob Ryan and his fellow travelers.

And why? Because Bob Ryan and the liberal sports media believe football "reflects poorly on us as a people." Their real charge against football is less about the people who play it and more about the people who watch it. If it takes a bunch of "borderline psychopaths" to play football, well then it must take *a nation* full of borderline, if not actual, psychopaths to turn it into the wealthiest sport in the country. Bob Ryan is saying it's not about him, or his fellow sports writers, it's about you. The fact that football is this country's "sport of choice" represents an inherent defect in you, me, and the country as a whole. The liberal sports media, like liberals in general, think America is fundamentally flawed, which is why traditional, conservative, Christian America is always in need of being reformed by progressives. Football, to them, can seem the ultimate expression of the unreformed American spirit—chauvinistic, competitive, and even too Christian, as football is so big in religious states like Texas and is more given to midfield prayers than any other sport.

This, in the minds of Bob Ryan and the leftist American sports media, is why football must go. And make no mistake about it: Bob Ryan knows that he's speaking on behalf of the sports media when he says these things. Pay careful attention to his words, "I suspect there are many more out there like me." Someone like Bob Ryan doesn't write that unless he knows *for a fact* that there are many more sports reporters and commentators out there who think the way he does. And then the less subtle, "*We* [emphasis added] are essentially troubled by the casual acceptance our society has of a sport that really and truly maims people." That's the voice of the liberal sports media.

How did we get to this point? I mean, for all of our lives, most of us "normal" people have been taught that football was America's game because it embodied everything that was great about America: the toughness, the grit, the will to succeed and win, the determination to see something through despite hardships and setbacks, the ability to work together as a team with people who don't look like you and strive toward a common goal. Isn't that, among other things, what makes America great? Isn't that what foreign people mean when they talk about that great, quintessentially American character trait, the "can-do spirit" that refuses to be denied? Football is the anvil upon which that steely American resolve has been forged. It's in our blood because it's part and parcel of who we are. Yet to the sports media, who should be, you might think, the most knowledgeable and passionate supporters of the game, it's a pox. It's a scourge that represents what's wrong with America, and therein lies the problem.

It's not just that the sports media get it wrong sometimes. That wouldn't be anywhere near as big of a problem, and it could be easily forgiven. No, it's that *their values and worldview* are completely different from those of most other people in the country. Most people see football as a sport that gives opportunities to poor kids who would otherwise not have them; the media see it as a tool for rich white owners to exploit the bodies and livelihoods of poor black kids to earn a buck. Most people understand that youth football is potentially dangerous, but they also understand, as Daniel Flynn points out in *The War on Football*, that football is actually less dangerous than skateboarding, bicycling, or skiing. Most of the media see it as a concussion factory, where kids are berated by coaches into trying to maim each other, just as in Malcolm Gladwell's dogfighting analogy. That's the worldview of the intelligentsia in the American sports media, and they've decided, in all their infinite wisdom, acting as the elitists that they are, to use their microphones, cameras, and keyboards to correct what they believe to be a mental defect in *our* minds. Lucky us, right? How thoughtful of them. The reality, of course, is something altogether different. The reality, as the NIOSH study proved, is that NFL players do not die faster than "normal" people. From *USA Today*: "A records-based study of retired [NFL] players conducted by the National Institute for Occupational Safety and Health (NIOSH) concludes that they have a much lower death rate than men in the general population, contrasting the notion that football players don't live as long."[20]

Nor do they suffer disproportionately from heart disease: "Yet the results also revealed that nearly 38% of deaths from the pool of retirees—who played at least five seasons between 1959 and 1988—were linked to heart disease. Even so, NIOSH concluded in the study that the risk of dying of heart disease for the retirees as an overall group is lower than that for the general population."[21]

As discussed earlier, through evidence provided by NIOSH and others, there is no evidence that NFL players commit suicide at elevated levels and no evidence that CTE is a direct cause of suicide. In fact, a study that went almost completely *unreported* by our "truth-seekers" in the press showed that there's no definitive link between contact sports and CTE at all. Dr. Stella Karantzoulis and Dr. Christopher Randolph of the Loyola University Medical Center—in other words, people who have forgotten more about the human brain than Malcolm

Gladwell will ever know—concluded that there was no link between football and increased risk of CTE: "Karantzoulis and Randolph examined symptoms of retired NFL players who had mild cognitive impairment and said that symptoms seen in the retired players were virtually the same as those observed in non-athletes. They write that these findings cast doubt on the notion that CTE is a novel condition unique to athletes who have experienced concussions."[22]

In their conclusion they said: "One cannot deny that boxing and other contact sports can potentially result in some type of injury to the brain. There currently are no carefully controlled data, however, to indicate a definitive association between sport-related concussion and increased risk for late-life cognitive and neuropsychiatric impairment of any form."[23]

I should have become aware of this study from Bob Ryan. I should have found out about it from Don Banks on the Monday Morning Quarterback. I should have heard about it from Malcolm Gladwell during one of his inexplicable appearances on ESPN.

But I didn't. Instead, I only found it while researching for this book. If the Loyola University study had shown that former NFL players were ten times more likely to die, commit suicide, grow a third nipple, or vote Republican, it's all I or any of us would have heard about for months. The sports media for the most part ignored the study because it contradicted their narrative. It flew in the face of their agenda to prove that football is a symptom of the disease that is American culture. Dan Wolken was right about one thing: the football-safety debate is indeed becoming like the climate-change debate, and the reports that show football *isn't* killing people are an inconvenient truth.

CHAPTER SEVEN

BLACKLISTING LIMBAUGH

Anyone's first time on air is nerve-racking, especially in radio. It's not like television, where you can blame the hair guy for making you look bad, or the graphics guy for having the wrong backdrop behind you. With all due respect to my brethren and sistren on the television side, I think radio is better. Simply put, it's all on you. If you fail, it's all you. If you succeed…it's all you as well. But no matter your venue, the first time on air is hard, especially when you know you're going to be diving into something controversial. It is one thing to say cutting, provocative, and insightful things to your steering wheel and quite another to say them into a working microphone with real people listening, people who might be genuinely angered by what you say.

And so it was, in October 2009, in the eye of the sharknado of controversy swirling around Rush Limbaugh's effort to purchase a share of the St. Louis Rams, that I was given my first shot at sports talk radio. The cohost I auditioned with that day, for reasons that are known only to him, had no interest in talking about Rush and told me not to bring it up. But there was a two- to three-minute gap in the show where he had to leave to do an update on one of our sister stations, and I knew that was going to be my chance. I was angry, and I wanted people to know why. And as soon as my cohost left, I let fly. I let fly about how hypocritical the players, specifically the black players, were for their condemnation of Limbaugh. Several black players had recently said they would not play for Limbaugh, citing quotations attributed to Limbaugh, some out of context, others completely fabricated, that they found to be "insensitive" and "disrespectful."

Though, interestingly, none of these players had ever said they wouldn't play alongside Michael Vick, who brutally maimed, tortured, and killed hundreds of dogs. None of these players had spoken harshly of Ray Lewis, who, although never proved guilty of murder, had certainly been hip-deep in a situation that resulted in the stabbing deaths of two young black males. Nor had anybody been this vocal about a player like Leonard Little, who through his own drunken negligence had killed an innocent mother of three with his car.

I then spoke of how different (read: better) a world we might live in if the black players angry at Rush Limbaugh saved their anger for the players who create the "thug" stereotype of black athletes in America. Maybe if the players made a point of disavowing the thugs, "thug life" wouldn't seem as cool as it does to too many kids.

Within seconds of that rant, all five phone lines lit up with callers, most of whom questioned my ancestry, and one guy announced that he would never listen to our station ever again. Soon after, I found out that I got the job. That only accelerated the flow of hate on message boards and chat rooms from other media people in Houston who often tried to hide their real identities and went off at length about how I should never be allowed near another microphone again, and how there was no place in sports radio for someone as "backward" as me. But the backlash wasn't really about me, it was about boogeymen: that something or someone that gets under your skin and terrorizes you and seems to exist only to freak you out. To me, that thing is an ocelot…and Russell Brand. But to the liberal sports media, it's Rush Limbaugh. He is their boogeyman: the guy who really sticks in their craw; a weird foreign substance that when introduced into their perfectly manicured liberal ecosystem causes a collapse of apocalyptic proportions. Which is why if you really want to understand the maelstrom of liberal media hissy-fitting that sprung up in the fall of 2009 when Limbaugh bid to become a part-owner of an NFL franchise, you really have to go back to the fall of 2003.

There actually was a time, however short-lived, when Limbaugh was allowed to circulate in the sports media gene pool. In 2003, Limbaugh was given a role on ESPN's pregame show, *Sunday NFL Countdown*. During the week-three edition of the show, Rush, along with panelists Chris Berman, Steve Young, Michael Irvin, and Tom Jackson, delved into the recent woes of Philadelphia Eagles quarterback Donovan McNabb. Not only had McNabb stunk it up in the NFC championship game the year before, but he had been a dumpster fire during the first two weeks of the regular season, and the panel was discussing the possible reasons why. It was then that Limbaugh did what anybody who had ever listened to Limbaugh could have told you he was going to do. And it was glorious: "Sorry to say this, I don't think he's been that good from the get-go," Limbaugh said. "I think what we've had here is a little social concern in the NFL. The media has been very desirous that a black quarterback do well. There is a little hope invested in McNabb, and he got a lot of credit for the performance of this team that he didn't deserve. The defense carried this team."[1]

Now, these comments were entirely true and accurate on all counts, which presented the sports media with a tremendous problem; namely, *Limbaugh's comments were entirely true and accurate on all counts.* You see, in a normal world, with an unbiased media interested in truth, only lies and inaccuracies would pose a threat. But, in our world, with a leftist, agenda-driven, race-mongering flash mob running the show, it is truth and accuracy that pose the threat, specifically, when the charges are levied at them.

A little background here. Despite being featured in dozens of one-on-one interviews, being tapped for NFL promotional pieces and commercials, landing major endorsement deals, and getting more face time on ESPN than most other athletes, Donovan McNabb was never among the five best quarterbacks in the league at any point in his career. In the 2003 season, the year that Limbaugh made these comments, McNabb was fourteenth in passing yards, seventeenth in touchdowns, and nineteenth in completion percentage out of thirty-two NFL quarterbacks.[2] Despite his playing in perhaps the most offense-friendly, pass-happy era in league history, McNabb never had a four-thousand-yard season, something that has come to be expected from elite NFL quarterbacks.

In other words, if you look up "Average NFL Quarterback" in the dictionary, there would be a huge, smiling picture of Donovan McNabb staring right back at you. If Donovan McNabb had been a white quarterback with those numbers, he never would have been featured on ESPN so regularly. That is, unless he had used the N-word or had come out as gay, in which case he would have been the *only* person on ESPN for about four months. But you line up Donovan

McNabb's production behind that of any quarterback in the league, white or black, and he would not have stood out.

In fact, it's debatable that McNabb was even the best *black* quarterback in the NFL in 2003. Daunte Culpepper, the late Steve McNair, and even Aaron Brooks all had better numbers than he did. So why did the sports media latch onto McNabb? Probably because the bulk of the American sports media are based in and around New York, and Donovan McNabb played just down the road, in Philly. After all, going to Tennessee to talk to Steve McNair or going to Louisiana to talk to Aaron Brooks would require our highly sophisticated and nuanced media elite to leave their Northeastern comfort zone and mingle with the commoners.

Limbaugh nailed two incredibly key points: (A) Donovan McNabb was never that good to begin with, and the fact that his team had advanced to the playoffs only reinforced Limbaugh's point that the defense carried the team; and (B) it was the sports media who had turned McNabb into something he was not. So how did the sports media deal with the issue of being publicly and accurately called out this way? Their position was completely indefensible; anyone can look up McNabb's numbers, compare them with the Eagles' success, and see that Limbaugh was right.

The sports media, instead of conceding that they had made way too much of McNabb, turned Limbaugh's comments into an attack on a *black quarterback*. Within forty-eight hours, the virtual entirety of the sports world, plus the political race machine, had converged on Limbaugh. Democratic presidential candidates Wesley Clark and Howard Dean were both reported as saying Limbaugh should be fired. Clark, a retired army general, called the remarks "hateful and ignorant speech."[3] The NAACP condemned Limbaugh's remarks, calling them "bigoted and ignorant," and called for the network to fire Limbaugh or at least provide an opposing point of view on the show.[4] "It is appalling that ESPN has to go to this extent to try to increase viewership," then–NAACP president Kweisi Mfume said in a statement.[5] The National Association of Black Journalists also called for ESPN to "separate itself" from Limbaugh. "ESPN's credibility as a journalism entity is at stake," NABJ president Herbert Lowe said in a news release. "It needs to send a clear signal that the subjects of race and equal opportunity are taken seriously at its news outlets."[6]

The NFL disclaimed any responsibility for Limbaugh's remarks. "ESPN knew what it was getting when they hired Rush Limbaugh," league vice president Joe Browne said. "ESPN selects its on-air talent, not the NFL."[7] Which brings up a good point: Why did ESPN hire Rush Limbaugh? Clearly they knew who he was. They knew his feelings on the media and the fact that he would not hold back. Sure, they wanted the ratings bump Limbaugh would give them (*Sunday NFL Countdown* ratings went up 10 percent with Limbaugh on the show),[8] but they had to know they couldn't just get the milk without buying the cow. In any event, it didn't end there. In an article titled "In No Rush to Forget," *New York Daily News* sports writer Ralph Vacchiano interviewed McNabb's father about what impact Limbaugh's comments had on him. Vacchiano's lead sentence was high comedy: "When Sam McNabb heard the words coming from Rush Limbaugh's mouth—the hateful, hurtful words about his son Donovan—he flashed back to another devastating night in the early 1980s."[9]

Hateful? Hurtful? Limbaugh's comments weren't about "his son Donovan"—they were about agenda-driven reporters like Ralph Vacchiano who hyped an average black quarterback into something that he wasn't. If anything is hateful or hurtful, it's that. But this is a perfect example of how the sports media convinced the public that Limbaugh had been criticizing black QBs instead of criticizing the sports media for overhyping black QBs.

In his next bit, Vacchiano told how McNabb's father likened Limbaugh's comments to an evening in the 1980s when his family's new home, purchased in a white neighborhood, was broken into and damaged by racist vandals. Really? Saying a black quarterback isn't very good is akin to vandals breaking into your home?

In a shocking twist, sports writer Allen Barra, writing in the liberal online magazine Slate, had the gumption to announce "Rush Limbaugh Was Right." His story appeared a week after Rush resigned from ESPN. Barra wrote:

> Limbaugh is being excoriated for making race an issue in the NFL. This is hypocrisy. I don't know of a football writer who didn't regard the dearth of black NFL quarterbacks as one of the most important issues in the late '80s and early '90s.
>
> So far, no black quarterback has been able to dominate a league in which the majority of the players are black. To pretend that many of us didn't want McNabb to be the best quarterback in the NFL because he's black is absurd. To say that we shouldn't root for a quarterback to win because he's black is every bit as nonsensical as to say that we shouldn't have rooted for Jackie Robinson to succeed because he was black....
>
> Consequently, it is equally absurd to say that the sports media haven't overrated Donovan McNabb because he's black. I'm sorry to have to say it; he is the quarterback for a team I root for. Instead of calling him overrated, I wish I could be admiring his Super Bowl rings. But the truth is

that I and a great many other sportswriters have chosen for the past few years to see McNabb as a better player than he has been because we *want* him to be.

Rush Limbaugh didn't say Donovan McNabb was a bad quarterback because he is black. He said that the media have overrated McNabb because he is black, and Limbaugh is right.[10]

But as noble as the effort was, Allen Barra was trying to plug the Hoover Dam with a toothpick. As asinine as the backlash against Limbaugh was, it had already worked. In fact, it worked well before the Vacchiano or Barra articles came out. Limbaugh stepped down from his role on *Sunday NFL Countdown* three days after making his comments about McNabb. Sports media, the mainstream media, Democrat political leaders, and the NAACP had worked in perfect synchronicity to force Limbaugh out.

I can already hear it: "But, Dylan! Are you saying that the sports media coordinated with Democrat politicians and the NAACP to bring down Limbaugh?!" No, what I'm saying is that no coordination was necessary, because they're all the same people and they all look at the world in the same way. They're all liberals, and together they succeeded in driving Limbaugh from their jealously guarded (and toxic) ecosystem…at least for the moment. Limbaugh's next attempt at "the fulfillment of a dream," to be involved in the sports world, came six years after McNabb-gate, when he tried to become part-owner of the St. Louis Rams.

In early October 2009, Limbaugh announced on his radio show that he and St. Louis Blues owner Dave Checketts had put together a bid to buy the St. Louis Rams. Mortified that the cunning (and rich) Limbaugh might circumvent their ecosystem's well-protected firewalls and buy his way into the NFL, the racial flash mob kicked into high gear. ESPN's Mike Wilbon even went on CNN's *Reliable Sources* with Howard Kurtz to rail against the conservative would-be owner. With the flash mob fully behind him, "Magic Mike" took center stage: "I don't know whether Rush Limbaugh is a straight-up bigot or he simply plays one on TV and radio, but he is universally reviled by black people in this country."[11]

Not only was Wilbon deluded in naming himself the spokesman for all black people, but he was majorly exaggerating. It's debatable whether Limbaugh was even "universally reviled" among black sportscasters. Stephen A. Smith (who is black) said in an interview on CNN that black players who said they wouldn't play for Limbaugh were "walking hypocrites."[12] He even said Rush's comments about McNabb in 2003 should have no bearing on his becoming an owner. As Smith said, "If he has the money, there's absolutely nothing wrong with it."[13]

The fact that Kurtz didn't challenge Wilbon's ludicrous exaggeration—given that Smith had made his comments on CNN less than a full week before Wilbon's claim that Limbaugh was "universally reviled"—was unfortunate. However, Kurtz did counter Wilbon on one important point; he just didn't go far enough. During a previous rant on *Pardon the Interruption*, Wilbon claimed that Rush had said incredibly hurtful and racist things on his show. Among them, that the NFL "too often looks like a game between the Crips and the Bloods without any weapons"[14] and that "slavery...had its merits."[15]

Kurtz called out Wilbon for attributing the slavery quotation to Limbaugh despite having no proof of when he supposedly said it. In fact, the source for this alleged quotation was a radical sociology professor from Georgetown University named Michael Eric Dyson, whom Limbaugh himself had called out on his radio show in September 2009:

"There's even a guy that was on MSNBC, I'm not going to play the sound bite for you. I am not going to dignify this by playing it, but it was this morning on MSNBC. This guy, *Michael Eric Dyson, claims that I have written that slavery was a good thing* [emphasis added]. Even Scarborough said, 'What are you talking about?' 'Oh, yeah, you can read it, you can read it.' I have never said slavery was a good thing!"[16]

Just how radical is Dyson? Here's what he had to say about Mumia Abu-Jamal, who murdered a Philadelphia police officer in 1981:

> So for me, then, the Mumia Abu-Jamal case is about the person who is able to articulate the interests of minority people not only in terms of color, but in terms of ideology. Because we know what the real deal here is also about. It is about the repression of left-wing, progressive, insightful cultural criticism and political and moral critique aimed at the dominant hegemonic processes of American capitalism and the American state as evidenced in its racist, imperialist and now we might add homophobic and certainly its patriarchal practices.[17]

So Abu-Jamal articulated the "interests of minority people" by killing a white cop? Is this the kind of critical insight it takes to be a professor at Georgetown nowadays? Dyson also waxed silly when asked what he thought Tupac would have to say about 9/11:

> I think that Tupac would say, "What business do we have being in Arab nations when the tentacles of colonialism and capitalism suck the lifeblood of native or indigenous

people?" … He would have had questions about who really was the thug. He would have said that America has ignored the vicious consequences of its imperialistic practices across the world. America ignores how millions of people suffer on a daily basis throughout the world, except in isolated spots that involve so-called national interests. Thirdly, that America has forfeited its duty as global policeman, by virtue of its own mistreatment of black people.[18]

Great! So Michael Wilbon's go-to source for cutting racial and sociological commentary and non-researched pull quotes is a Marxist, racist, anti-American hack at Georgetown University. Wilbon wasn't the only one who cited Dyson's made-up Rush quotation either; *Detroit Free Press* sportswriter Drew Sharp took the Dyson-generated lie and used it in an article in which he tried to stop Limbaugh's bid to become an NFL owner: "Pittsburgh Steelers linebacker James Farrior agreed Sunday that nobody with Limbaugh's litany of incendiary racial comments—Limbaugh once said on his nationally syndicated radio show that slavery 'had its merits'—deserves the privilege of owning an NFL franchise."[19]

The bogus quotation, by this point, had also made it onto Rush's *Wikipedia* page. So Sharp either heard this directly from Dyson, from Wilbon, or from related misguided commentary, or he latched onto a news source that, as Debbie Schlussel once put it, is "less reliable than the Onion." What does it say when Drew Sharp and Michael Wilbon use as their source material a quack professor who is to the left of Che Guevara and then never bother to check the quotation— you know, fact-checking? Well, really it tells you just about everything. Yes, the liberal mainstream media are biased in sometimes crazy ways, but so are sports media.

The players, who were as much tools of the media as anyone, were beyond ridiculous in the Limbaugh saga as well. As Mathias Kiwanuka of the New York Giants put it:

> I don't want anything to do with a team that he has any part of. He can do whatever he wants, it is a free country. But if it goes through, I can tell you where I am not going to play. I am not going to draw a conclusion from a person off of one comment, but when it is time after time after time and there's a consistent pattern of disrespect and just a complete misunderstanding of an entire culture that I am a part of, I can't respect him as a man.... It is just an opinion show that should be only be taken for shock value. I liken it to *South Park* when I am listening to him.[20]

If I had a dollar for every minute that Mathias Kiwanuka listened to Rush Limbaugh, I bet I'd be no richer. Kiwanuka and other players were spun by the media and they stayed spun, convinced that Rush was a hater, when the real hater was the liberal sports media that hate Rush.

Jets linebacker Bart Scott said, "It's an oxymoron that he criticized Donovan McNabb. A lot of us took it as more of a racial-type thing. I can only imagine how his players would feel. I know I wouldn't want to play for him. He's a jerk. He's an —. What he said [about McNabb] was inappropriate and insensitive, totally off-base. He could offer me whatever he wanted, I wouldn't play for him.... I wouldn't play for Rush Limbaugh. My principles are greater and I can't be bought."[21]

After looking up the definition of oxymoron so he can actually use it correctly next time, Scott should have done a little research into what Rush actually said instead of what the media had told him he said. Beyond that, whatever Scott thinks, Stephen A. Smith absolutely nailed it when he noted that players go where the money is, and almost all allegedly anti-Rush players would probably be happy hypocrites if Rush owned a team and offered them a bigger paycheck to play on it.

But it's not misguided players who are the issue: it's the sports media and a little something called objective consistency. I'm too cynical and scarred by my experiences in journalism to expect fairness or honesty. I mean, you're getting that in this book. But this book is about *what's wrong* with the sports media, not about what's right. So maybe one day we can strive for and reach consistency. Here would have been a great place to start. In June 2012 it was announced that Bill Maher, the radical, left-wing, religion-baiting host of *Real Time with Bill Maher* on HBO, had bought a minority stake in the New York Mets. Except I was the one who included "radical, left-wing, religion-baiting host," because nowhere in any of the very few articles that reported this transaction did the sports media accurately portray who Maher is. In the Huffington Post Sports article about the purchase, Maher is referred to as a "stand-up comic, and a political satirist,"[22] which makes him sound about as threatening as a harmless circus clown.

The ESPN.com article announcing the ownership venture referred to Maher as a "political commentator."[23] The ESPN.com article announcing Limbaugh's attempt to buy the Rams referred to him as a "conservative," and the "voice of the Republican Party."[24] One of these things is not like the other. Now, for those of you not in the know, Bill Maher is every bit as liberal as Rush Limbaugh is conservative, except he's about eleven times more vulgar, crass, and offensive than Limbaugh could ever be on his worst day. When Rush

Limbaugh announced his intent to become a minority owner of the
St. Louis Rams, *New York Times* sports columnist George Vecsey
did everything short of calling Limbaugh an outright racist, referring
to him as "a virulent exhibitionist" who uses racist "code words" to
communicate with his "constituency" and has a "visceral" hatred of
President Obama.[25]

But when the *Times* reported on Maher's acquisition of a minority share of the Mets, Maher was described as "the most celebrated
person—at least the only one with a TV show—known to have
become a new partner in the team with the Wilpon family...."[26]
Hmmm. That's quite a change from visceral, racist-code-word guy.
But they went even further than that. Attempting to insulate Maher
from any criticism over the tons of crazy and insulting things he has
said over the years, the *Times* went on to describe Maher as a person
whose "libertarianism and atheistic views are elements of his comedy."[27] You see? He doesn't really mean it! Because if you say horrible
and offensive things on TV or on stage at a comedy joint, it doesn't
really count! Somewhere Michael Richards is shedding a tear. What
are some of the awful things said by Maher over the years? In October 2007, while on his previous show *Politically Incorrect*, Maher
likened retarded children to dogs: "But I've often said that if I had—I
have two dogs—if I had two retarded children, I'd be a hero. And yet
the dogs, which are pretty much the same thing. What? They're sweet.
They're loving. They're kind, but they don't mentally advance at all....
Dogs are like retarded children."[28]

As if that weren't bad enough, one of his guests said that she had
a nine-year-old nephew who was retarded and that she never thought
of him as a dog. Maher, instead of taking this golden opportunity to
remove his head from his ass, turned to the woman who had never

looked at her nephew as being a canine before and said, "Maybe you should."[29]

The Catholic League has even compiled an annotated list, ranging from 1998 to the middle of 2014, of anti-Catholic venom from Maher, not that anyone in sports media cares about that. Race, though, is something they do care about, and even here Maher gets a free pass, as all liberals do.

In May 2010, while talking about the BP oil spill, Maher gave us insight into what he thinks a real black man is, and what a real black president should be like: "I thought when we elected a black president, we were going to get a black president. You know, this [BP oil spill] is where I want a real black president. I want him in a meeting with the BP CEOs, you know, where he lifts up his shirt so you can see the gun in his pants. That's...[in black man voice] 'We've got a motherfucking problem here?'—and shoot somebody in the foot."[30]

Yeah, that's way better than saying you don't think Donovan McNabb is a very good quarterback. Rush Limbaugh merely said a black guy wasn't a very good quarterback, not because he was black, but based on his playing record. He blamed *the media* for having a racial angle, which was patently obvious to everybody, and suddenly he is full of "visceral" hatred and is a "virulent exhibitionist." Bill Maher stereotypes black men as gangster thugs and that's okay, because after all Maher is just a "satirist" who blends atheism and libertarianism in with his comedy and is the "most celebrated person" to have become a partner with the Wilpon family. How quaint.

There are dozens of other examples of Maher's racial insensitivity, but I think you get the picture. I have no issue with Bill Maher's buying a share of a baseball team. I find the words he chooses to say completely vile and contemptible in almost every way, but he still has a right to buy a professional sports team. And so did Rush Limbaugh. Both Limbaugh and Maher represent opposite ends of the political spectrum, but the "objective" sports media had an obligation to treat them the same way, and they didn't. Because the sports media are not objective, not even close.

CHAPTER EIGHT

BULL IN DURHAM

Ah, lacrosse. They very thought of it conjurcs up images of regal exploits on the lush green fields of our country's finest institutions, as young men, primarily affluent young men, play the game handed down to them by our Indian forebears. But if you're a member of the mainstream media, especially the mainstream sports media, it might conjure up a very different image—a very drunk, very violent, and very rapey image, where those same young lads of wealth and privilege abuse their position and exploit the helpless and vulnerable minorities who serve them.

How do I know the sports media have this image? Because that's precisely the image they tried to sell us in 2006, when a stripper named Crystal Mangum accused three Duke University lacrosse team members of forcing her into a bathroom, beating her, raping her, and sodomizing her. The evidence against the players was so flimsy that it folded like a pre-fab in a cat-five hurricane, but that didn't stop the media. Within five days of the arrests of two Duke players (a third would be charged later), there were 673 news stories, including 160 from major television news outlets, talking about the alleged rape that had occurred at an off-campus house party. Right now you're thinking to yourself: *Geez, almost seven hundred news stories about a couple of lacrosse players who* might *have raped a stripper? That seems like a lot.*

Oh, I'm sorry. Did I happen to mention that the stripper was black and the lacrosse players were white? My bad. I guess race isn't always the first thing I look at; after all, this isn't ESPN's *Pardon the Interruption.* But it didn't take long for the racial flash mob to belly up to this bar. All over the country, the story went out: privileged white lacrosse players at a prestigious college rape underprivileged young black woman. It was the stuff of legend for the media, sports and mainstream alike. Over and over again the media told us that lacrosse players were a pampered, privileged, and, as a consequence, abusive elite. After the case against the Duke players fell apart, reporter Terry Moran took to ABC's website to remind us not to feel sorry for these wealthy and spoiled white boys who had just had their names dragged through the mud by a frenzied media:

> As students of Duke University or other elite institutions, these young men will get on with their privileged lives. There is a very large cushion under them—the one that softens the blows of life for most of those who go to Duke or similar places, and have connections through family, friends and school to all kinds of prospects for success. They are very differently situated in life from, say, the young women of the Rutgers University women's basketball team.[1]

Way to go, Ter. God forbid any culpability be admitted on the part of the media for doing virtually no investigative work despite having armies of reporters camped out in Durham, North Carolina, for the better part of a year. No, instead the message was, "Hey, don't you dare feel sorry for the kids we slandered, even though we had no evidence whatsoever of their supposed guilt. They're rich, they're white, they're evil, they're elitists, they deserve it!" (By the way, ABC's Terry Moran went to college at an exclusive and extremely expensive music conservatory in Wisconsin. So, any time you want to fire him, go ahead: there is a very large cushion under him.)

Look again at what Moran said: he's acting as if these guys are still guilty. That blog posting was written *after* we found out that his reporting, and the rest of the mainstream media's reporting on the case, was completely bogus. Yet you read what he wrote there and you get the impression that he feels like the Duke players got away with something. As if, despite being cleared and exonerated of any and all wrongdoing, the Duke players aren't any less guilty now than they were before. That's because to the media, the wealth and privilege of the Duke lacrosse players *were* their real crime. The accusation of rape was bad (even though it turned out to be false), but the alleged rape was just the pretext for allowing the media to swoop in and expose just how spoiled, violent, abusive, and racist these children of privilege really are. And the media weren't in the least bit interested in the mounting number of facts that proved the case against the players was made up, because the case already confirmed the way the sports media see the world: rich, evil, and spoiled white people abusing defenseless, helpless, and vulnerable black people. The end.

What's that they say? *Never let the facts get in the way of a good story?* You better believe it. Two points need to be made here before we go any further: I will not rehash the entire saga of how the media screwed up the Duke lacrosse story, because (A) that would take entirely too long, considering it was quite possibly the worst-managed affair in the history of the American media; and (B) one neglected aspect of the story, which I want to explore here, is how the media believed they did nothing wrong in reporting the events *as they saw them* (instead of as they were) in Durham, North Carolina, and actually promoted some of the worst offenders to positions of greater power *after* their stories were thoroughly debunked by the facts. This is true both for the sports reporters who got it wrong and mainstream media idiots like Terry Moran, which underlines one of the most important points of this book: *there is no difference between the sports media and the mainstream media.* Both are rabidly liberal, and both see the world and the stories they cover through a prism of "social justice" that colors everything they report. The subject matter they cover differs, but the way they cover it doesn't.

Let me to introduce you to John Feinstein, sports columnist for the *Washington Post*, who in May 2007, while on the nationally syndicated *Jim Rome Show*, said that he felt the Duke lacrosse players were "guilty of everything but rape" and "I really don't want to hear that they're victims and martyrs, and that their lives have been ruined."[2] Hmmm, guilty of everything but rape? That's funny; rape and sodomy, along with battery, were the only things the players were charged with, and in May 2007, Feinstein and everyone else in the world knew those charges were bogus. So what else could they possibly have been guilty of? Answer: The same thing that Terry Moran found them guilty of—being rich while white. In fact, so unhinged was Feinstein that in March 2006 when the Duke lacrosse story first broke and details of what actually happened were sketchy at best, Feinstein told ESPN's Tony Kornheiser that the whole lacrosse team should be done away with: "You know, I don't want to hear any ifs, ands, or buts. These kids have acted disgracefully, just by the fact that not one of them—I don't want to hear about the code among buddies and among teams. A crime was committed. There were witnesses to the crime. They need to come forward and say what they saw.... They won't, and that's why I'm saying the hell with them—strip their scholarships."[3]

Feinstein actually wanted forty-seven athletes, one of whom was black (and could not have met Mangum's description of the rapists, because she said all three were white), stripped of their scholarships. And why? Because none of them would confess to witnessing a crime that had never happened! This despite the fact that only days before Feinstein uttered his tripe on national television it had been reported that three Duke lacrosse team captains had come forward, told police exactly what had happened, and even *volunteered to be polygraphed* in order to prove the stripper was a liar. But none of this mattered to Feinstein or Moran, because to them the players were guilty of living lives of privilege and partying while white. The media condemned the players *just for who they were*—or not even that, just for the media's image of them.

Terry Moran and John Feinstein are different types of reporters. One of them works for a large mainstream news conglomerate covering major news stories around the world. The other works for a newspaper covering sports. And yet when their worlds converged in the Duke lacrosse case, they saw the story in exactly the same (and factually wrong) way. Like Moran, Feinstein was contemptuous of the idea that these young men's futures might be harmed by irresponsible media commentary and outright slander. He did not care, because they were children of wealth and privilege. Guilt or innocence was irrelevant; what mattered was that those rich white kids had more wealth and power than other kids do, and that was wrong.

Nothing infuriates the liberal media more. Especially because most media people come from privileged backgrounds as well, and lashing out at others of their class (especially those they might imagine are conservative in a preppy sort of way) is how they assuage the massive insecurities, pangs of guilt, and self-loathing they have about their own upbringing.

Add the racial element on top of that: lacrosse players lustily ogling poor black strippers while wearing their Dockers and J. Crew shirts and drinking their beer and living the good life at the "Harvard of the South," and you had liberal sports writers practically soiling themselves as they raced to their laptops to get on record trashing these kids. Damn the facts and evidence; someone had to pay for this post–Jim Crow outrage, and the accused players would be lambs in the liberal-media slaughter.

The unquestioned leader of the liberal media lynch mob against the players was then–*New York Times* sports columnist Selena Roberts. When Durham district attorney Mike Nifong, now disgraced and disbarred, was tossing as much red meat as possible to the media to gin up support for his completely fraudulent case against the players, no member of the fourth estate gobbled it up and asked for seconds more than Selena Roberts.

Like the rest of the media fraternity, Roberts assumed the players were guilty. On March 31, 2006, writing in the *New York Times*, Roberts claimed: "Players have been forced to give up their DNA, but to the dismay of investigators, none have come forward to reveal an eyewitness account."[4] This was three days *after* the lacrosse team captains released their statement, dated March 28, 2006, where they made clear that not only were they fully cooperating with the police but that no rape or sexual assault had occurred. In other words, Roberts was condemning the players for not stepping forward and providing an eyewitness account *of something that never happened.* And that something that never happened was later *proved,* in a court of law, not to have happened. Right now, I am making my shocked face.

In an interview with the sports website The Big Lead about her article, Roberts let her liberal freak flag fly and reminded us what her real issue was: "Basically, I wrote that a crime didn't have to occur for us to inspect the irrefutable evidence of misogyny and race baiting that went on that night.... Obviously, some segments of the Duke lacrosse crowd did not enjoy the scrutiny of their world."[5]

Question: What sort of "scrutiny" do you get when you're "investigated" by a reporter who has decided that you're guilty even if you're not?

Answer: Maybe the sort of scrutiny of a "reporter" who has decided that you are part of "a group of privileged players of fine pedigree entangled in a night that threatens to belie their status as human beings.... [Mixed metaphor alert:] Whatever the root, there is a common thread: a desire for teammates to exploit the vulnerable without heeding a conscience."[6]

Uh-huh. So the Duke lacrosse players might be subhuman beings without conscience. Who, one might ask, is exploiting whom here? The players who were innocent of all charges or a "reporter" who levels crazy-ass accusations likes this, which come not from the facts of the case but straight out of Progressive Ideology 101? The *facts* of the case did not move Roberts to make any sort of retraction or apology, because she believed that the "culture" of the Duke lacrosse players was inherently guilty of, um, er, not being progressive. "People want to conflate the crime and the culture,"[7] said the woman who did exactly that, accusing the culture of Duke lacrosse of giving birth to a nonexistent crime. "They want to say a crime did not happen, so therefore the culture that existed around that party did not happen."[8] Actually, what "they" are saying is that you got your story wrong, Selena Roberts, and you refuse to admit it, because you are an ideologue rather than a reporter.

What the Duke lacrosse case proved more than anything was that the media believe privileged, heterosexual white males are the true perpetrators of injustice, not the female minority stripper who happened to be lying (and who later, in a separate case, was convicted of murdering her boyfriend). Selena Roberts actually doubled down on her smearing of the innocent Duke lacrosse players and their university when she wrote: "Don't mess with Duke, though. To shine a light on its integrity has been treated by the irrational mighty as a threat to white privilege. Feel free to excoriate the African-American basketball stars and football behemoths for the misdeeds of all athletes, but lay off the lacrosse pipeline to Wall Street, excuse the khaki-pants crowd of SAT wonder kids."[9] Outside of Selena Roberts's progressive fantasy world, no one was defending "white privilege"; they were defending innocent players falsely accused of a heinous crime by a liar who had the media acting as her willing accomplices.

In late January 2007, as ethics charges piled up against the corrupt Durham district attorney Mike Nifong, feminist blogger Amanda Marcotte launched into a screed that would have made Al Sharpton blush:

> In the meantime, I've been sort of casually listening to CNN blaring throughout the waiting area and good fucking god is that channel pure evil. For a while, I had to listen to how the poor dear lacrosse players at Duke are being persecuted just because they held someone down and fucked her against her will—not rape, of course, because

the charges have been thrown out. Can't a few white boys sexually assault a black woman anymore without people getting all wound up about it? So unfair.[10]

The point here is not that Amanda Marcotte is a feminist, extremist whacko. The point is that if you clean up the language so that it's suitable for a newspaper, her view of the case was the same as that of Selena Roberts, who went from completely messing up this story for the *New York Times* to a multiple-six-figure job writing for *Sports Illustrated*. Just like Moran and Feinstein earlier, Marcotte and Roberts are in different fields. Yet both are feminist activists without a shred of difference between their respective views on men and race. Both Marcotte and Roberts mocked those who felt sorry for the players whose reputations had been trashed; both cited white privilege as the reason why players were "getting away with it."

Even worse for those of us who have any hope for journalistic integrity is that the *New York Times* allowed Roberts's reports to proceed in this way, sometimes with wild factual errors that were only belatedly corrected—if at all.[11] The *Times* had no issue with some of Roberts's other errors of fact (including incorrect reporting of the medical evidence). Nor did the *Times* have any problem with her race-baiting, her charges of misogyny, or her unfounded condemnation of the players, because as liberal media members themselves, they thought the same things about the players that Roberts did. Don't believe me? Let's look at what happened to Selena Roberts after the Duke lacrosse story.

Here you have a writer who couldn't have been more wrong about what happened at Duke, and who never even came close to apologizing, much less printing a retraction. In Normalsville, that would be the end of a reporter's career. You were maliciously and outspokenly wrong about a case of national prominence while working for the most famous newspaper in the land? Fired.

But instead of her career going up in a ball of flames as it should have after her "reporting" on the Duke lacrosse case, Selena, like Darth Vader, came back more powerful than we could possibly imagine. After leaving the *New York Times*, Roberts joined a group of writers at *Sports Illustrated* who replaced Rick Reilly on the magazine's then-popular back page.

As reported in *Deadspin* in 2009, Roberts and a colleague broke the story that Alex Rodriguez had tested positive for steroids in 2003. Terry McDonnell, *Sports Illustrated*'s managing editor at the time, called it the "biggest news break" in his tenure at the magazine.[12] Only days after the release of Roberts's book detailing A-Rod's positive steroid test, other media accolades started pouring in (per the Huffington Post):

> Selena Roberts is a "top-flight reporter," says *SI*'s Jeff Pearlman. (Feb. 10[, 2009])
>
> Roberts is "universally respected," agrees ESPN's Jayson Stark. (Feb. 17[, 2009])
>
> She is a "reporter who has conducted herself with nothing but class her entire career," says the *NY Daily News*' Mark Feinsand. (Feb. 17[, 2009])
>
> "I am friendly with Selena and consider her an excellent reporter," writes Joel Sherman of the *NY Post*. "I have no doubt she was tireless and diligent in this reporting, and— therefore—I suspect that what is in this book is accurate." (April 30[, 2009])[13]

This is beyond insane. A "reporter who has conducted herself with nothing but class her entire career"? Whatever Mark Feinsand was smoking when giving that comment is probably legal only in Colorado and Washington State. This woman had been an absolute joke when it came to her reporting on the only issue she ever covered that mattered: a veritable font of race-mucking, feminist angst, unfounded accusations, and innuendo. But she was A-OK with the "good ol' boy" network in the liberal sports media; she had been the good soldier, she had been the spokeswoman for everything they believed and wanted to say, and after that she could do no wrong.

Roberts was breathtakingly insightful and truthful about one thing, though. When being interviewed on the *Jim Rome Show* about her reporting on the Duke case, Roberts offered this defense: "I wrote about the culture at Duke, and there's no doubt about that. I stand by that today. I separated the criminal investigation from the culture."[14]

In fact, she didn't. Roberts's condemning articles could not have been written by anyone who believed the Duke players to be innocent. But there is this shred of truth to what she says about "culture." If the Duke allegations had occurred at Northern Illinois University, they wouldn't have attracted half the national attention that they did. The media, sports and mainstream, loved the Duke lacrosse story because it gave them a chance to attack a culture that they loathe and despise: the culture of affluent, *Southern* (read: conservative) white males. The mainstream and sports media did not converge on Duke to report on a rape. Guilt and innocence had already been determined by the media; they went there to attack a culture, to expose and destroy a culture they believe is racist, sexist, and inherently geared toward the wealthy and privileged—a culture that is antithetical to their liberal vision. The black stripper was just a stage prop.

The media's racial double standard would be plainly evident in future cases as well. In 2013, sexual assault allegations would arise about then–Heisman Trophy hopeful Jameis Winston (who is black) after a Florida State student claimed that Winston had raped her. The differences in the way the two cases were handled couldn't be more striking. The case against Winston was first filed in December 2012. It didn't reach the DA's office until December 2013, *a full year later.* By contrast, *only one month and three days after* Crystal Mangum said she was raped, the Duke lacrosse players (who were white) were being indicted by a grand jury. More important, the media coverage was totally different. There was a healthy debate but no rush to judge what had happened in the Winston case. On my show, and others, the debate was "if he's guilty," this should happen, or, "if they prove him guilty," he shouldn't win the Heisman.

In the Duke case, though, there had been no "what ifs" or "until there's proof." The debate was over how hard the Duke players should be punished, not whether they were guilty. In fact, the calls for punishment of the Duke players continued even after we knew they were innocent. This double standard prompted former Major League pitcher John Rocker to ask the most important question, in an article titled "What If Jameis Winston Were a White Lacrosse Player" on WND.com:

> Let's imagine that Jameis Winston isn't black, or the star football player for the Seminoles. Let's imagine that he is instead a white lacrosse player, who happens to play for Duke. Let's say an allegation emerges that he might have raped somebody. Do you think the student body and the school's fans would rally to his support? Do you think that the Durham Police Department would've sat on his case for nearly a year before sending it to the district attorney? Do you think police would've made veiled threats against the accuser for deciding to press charges? Would the district attorney carefully deliberate the case?

The likely answer to all of these questions would be no. And if the accuser were black, this story would be another racially charged national news case, and Winston would be portrayed as a modern-day Klansman by the national media, or the reincarnation of the Duke lacrosse players.

So why were the two cases portrayed so differently by the media and pursued so differently by the authorities? I can't say for sure, but I'm sure if Winston looked a lot more like the average Duke lacrosse player, we'd hear a different story than the one that is currently being pushed by the media.[15]

You could bet the farm on it. In fact, so different was the coverage of the Winston case from the Duke lacrosse case that ESPN went out of its way to assuage the liberal-feminist component in the sports media, and within their own network, by hosting a special impact segment after the Florida DA had announced that he wasn't pressing charges against Winston. The subject of said impact segment? The difficulties women face in coming forward after rapes and sexual assaults, and the ways such cases are handled by investigators and other law enforcement officials. In the first minute of the segment, host David Lloyd cited a number from the National Sexual Violence Resource Center which stated that only 2 to 10 percent of rape claims turn out to be false.[16] Mind you, this special aired shortly after Jameis Winston was cleared of any rape charges because the Florida DA couldn't find enough evidence to bring a case forward.

So why would ESPN air this discussion right after Winston had been exonerated, citing statistics that remind you that the overwhelming number of rape cases brought forward are true, and talking about how hard law enforcement makes it for women to come forward and talk about rape? It's because they wanted to cover their liberal behinds with their feminist fellow travelers.

ESPN radio hosts Colin Cowherd and Paul Finebaum appeared on the show. Cowherd strongly criticized the Florida state attorney for not understanding the seriousness of the case and the charge, as shown by the fact that he laughed through his press conference. Finebaum criticized the prosecutor for "grandstanding" and really went after Jameis Winston's attorney Tim Jansen for making "a mockery of the whole system, particularly with women." Finebaum also condemned the Tallahassee Police Department for their mishandling of the case.[17]

I agree with Finebaum on all of that: the Tallahassee Police Department did appear to bungle the investigation into the allegations against Winston, *and* the Florida district attorney did appear to be grandstanding. But similar criticisms could be made in the Duke lacrosse case where the prosecutor was grandstanding so much that he ended up getting disbarred. Yet ESPN didn't follow up the Duke lacrosse case with a special for the unjustly maligned players, lamenting how hard it was for them, and how hard it would be for them going forward. They didn't lay into the Durham Police Department for their mishandling of the case, and they certainly didn't criticize anyone in the media, which acted as a lynch mob, plain and simple, condemning the players merely because their accuser was black and because they decided Duke lacrosse players represented evil, wealthy, Southern, white males.

You can fault, if you want, the Duke lacrosse team for getting involved at all with a stripper. But it's not a criminal act, and it's not unknown for young men to do stupid things. But what is ironic is that the liberal media, so keen to promote any and all forms non-Christian sexuality—premarital sex, homosexual sex, "sex week" at major colleges, coed dorms and bathrooms that promote the hook-up culture, you mention it, they're for it—suddenly get all puritanical when it comes to something like this. That's because the sports media—like the mainstream liberal media—view every issue with an obsession on race, sex, and class. And if there's ever any opportunity to dump on rich white males and run to the support of poor black females, even if they're liars, they'll do it every time.

The most mind-blowing part of the liberal sports media's complete fail at covering the Duke lacrosse case was not that normal everyday analysts and writers ignored facts and made baseless claims—they do that all the time—but that even the so-called legal "experts" in the sports media made these mistakes.

Lester Munson currently writes and reports for ESPN.com and specializes in legal affairs. During the Duke lacrosse scandal, though, he worked for CNNSI.com, where he offered his not-so-learned advice. Munson went about wasting no opportunity to besmirch any credible evidence that might exonerate the lacrosse players, even searching for new and increasingly absurd ways for them to appear guiltier.

As chronicled on Brooklyn College historian KC Johnson's blog *Durham-in-Wonderland*, arguably the most authoritative historical account of the lacrosse scandal (outside this one, of course), Johnson describes Munson's appearance on the scene thusly:

> Munson's first case-related comments came on April 18. Despite the court filing from Mike Nifong's office that DNA would exonerate the innocent, Munson immediately downplayed DNA's role. "There are hundreds of convicted rapists in prison," he contended, "even though there was no sign of their DNA in the examinations of their victims...Lawyers for the accused players can talk endlessly about DNA, but the absence of DNA is not conclusive by

itself." He implied that the team had a history of "previous predatory conduct," and expressed little doubt that a crime occurred: "There is always an element of brutality in what occurs. In the Duke situation, it may be the number of athletes joining in the attack. In the Tyson case, the attack was brutal."[18]

So here you have Munson going even a level beyond the already beyond-awful Mike Nifong. Munson is so unhinged that he immediately refutes the notion put forth by Nifong that the DNA evidence could clear the innocent by telling us of "hundreds of convicted rapists" in jail today absent any DNA evidence against them.

And you know what? Technically, he's right. There are rapists who have been convicted without DNA evidence. Wouldn't, though, the absence of any DNA evidence in this case at least cause the objective, non-agenda-driven person to take some level of pause and question the air-tightness of the case against the players? Apparently not for Munson, who seems to have the case, and the guilt of the players, all sewn up.

Doubling down on the presumed guilt of the innocent, Lester Munson next removed any reasonable doubt about lacrosse player Reade Seligmann's innocence by construing his alibi as tantamount to an admission of guilt. The interviewer with CNNSI.com asked Munson: "A report has surfaced that one of the players charged, Reade Seligmann, has an alibi—including ATM receipts, a statement from a cab driver and evidence he was at his dormitory—indicating he had left the party before the alleged incident happened. Is this credible evidence?"[19]

After conceding the *potential* that Seligmann's alibi could prove his innocence, Munson went on to state that Seligmann might even be *guiltier*: "The police and the prosecutor will scrutinize this evidence in exquisite detail, and if they find something is askew, that something doesn't fit in the alibi evidence, they will not hesitate to charge Seligmann with yet another crime. That would be obstruction of justice."[20]

In any normal world, this response would have led to Munson's disbarring, or to dis-whatever happens to people who only "practice" law on TV. Note how the possibility that the alibi evidence could prove Seligmann's innocence only takes up about 4 percent of Munson's response here. He uses the remainder to cast the shadow of doubt.

Again, Seligmann's alibi evidence included an ATM receipt and a taxi driver's statement. ATMs have time-stamped receipts and also have security cameras. In fact, the ATM Seligmann used happened to capture him on camera at the exact time the alleged rape occurred. Not to mention the word of the cab driver to corroborate Seligmann's story.

For Munson to sit there and treat this evidence that Seligmann was innocent as somehow irrelevant, or worse—somehow putting him at risk of conviction for an additional crime—betrays a strong bias against the accused to say the least. Munson wasn't shy about revealing his bias: "You don't see many alibis in criminal cases—it's a very rare thing. Ordinarily, 99 times out of 100, the police have the right guy, and you'll find that most people arrested were involved in something. Getting the wrong guy is very unusual."[21]

Evidence for this claim was not forthcoming; of course neither was evidence for Mike Nifong's claims. None of that seemed to bother Munson. In his appearance on *Nancy Grace*, Munson was asked by Grace:

> GRACE: A lot has been said that the state doesn't have much of a case. Agree or disagree?

MUNSON: I disagree. I think the state has probably a better
case than most observers are describing. I have studied this
at some length for the piece that we had in Sports Illustrated
this week.

Mr. Nifong is a seasoned, experienced prosecutor. He
is not stupid. He's been doing this kind of thing for 30
years. I believe he has enough to make a prima facie case.
A jury will determine the guilt or the innocence of these
student athletes from Duke University. And I think that
Nifong is probably managing the discovery in such a way
that there may be some surprises for these defense lawyers
further down the road.[22]

Carefully note how Munson essentially says nothing here. How
does Nifong's thirty years on the job bolster his case? Dan Rather had
reported the news for more than thirty years and still ran with a
completely fabricated story to try to prevent the reelection of President
George W. Bush. So instead of actually answering the question about
the strength of Nifong's case, Munson instead gave us Nifong's résumé
and a little Civics 101 about how a jury will decide the case—and
unknowingly betrayed that he had no idea what he was talking about.
Though Nifong's case appeared weak, Munson assured Nancy Grace
that Nifong was probably "managing discovery in such a way that
there may be some surprises for these defense lawyers further down
the road."

There was only one problem with this: North Carolina is an open-
discovery state,[23] meaning that Mike Nifong was not allowed to
"manage discovery" with the goal of springing "surprises" against
defense attorneys later in trial. He was compelled by law to share any
and all information and evidence he had, at the defense's request. I

wouldn't expect Selena Roberts or Bomani Jones or John Feinstein or some other strictly sports talking head to know that information. But it does tell you something about sports reporters with "legal expert" in their title—namely that they really aren't.

Munson also proved unconvincing when Nancy Grace challenged him on the "victim's" credibility:

> GRACE: Back to Lester Munson with *Sports Illustrated*. What supports the victim account? And I know there's problems with the state's case. I'm not denying that, all right? You've got the second dancer who's given three or four different stories. But what supports the actual alleged victim's account, Lester?
> MUNSON: There is some veracity to the victim's account. She and the other woman, obviously, felt the sense of danger, a sense of menace in that house. They left a lot of stuff behind. They were able to describe what they left behind to the police, and the police, when they went to search the house, found everything there that the woman had described as left behind when she left in a big hurry in fear.[24]

Really? Three kids should spend the next twenty to thirty years behind bars because a couple of strippers left behind "a lot of stuff" at a house party? You'd think a lawyer might recognize that leaving stuff behind proves that you were at a location and that you left. It doesn't prove *why* you left, or how you *felt* when you were leaving, and if your case is based solely on that, you don't have a case.

Munson could never quite grasp Nifong's lack of a case. After Nifong dropped the charges against the players, *Sports Illustrated* for some reason went back to their reporter who had gotten just about everything wrong and asked him what was next for the players.

> MUNSON: They still face some serious charges. There is little doubt that something unsavory happened at the party on March 13. After the dismissal of the rape charges, it will be easier for the accused players to attempt to settle everything with a guilty plea on lesser charges. The likelihood of a trial on any of these charges is now greatly reduced.[25]

Something "unsavory"? Something unsavory accurately describes my nightlife from the age of about nineteen to twenty-two, and I can assure you that a rather large gulf exists between unsavory and rape. Note how Munson still, even in light of the dropping of the charges, still believes the players should plead guilty. Why?

Because the guilt of these players existed in the minds of Munson and the rest of the liberal media regardless of proof to the contrary. Unlike the usual sports reporters who spout opinions in legal cases without knowing anything about the law, Lester Munson *is* a lawyer and presumably should have known at some point that Nifong's case would fold like paper under any kind of serious scrutiny. Yet he stuck by the players' guilt—of something—long after the truth became obvious.

Somehow, though, this case did not discredit Munson as a "legal expert." In fact, like Selena Roberts, this episode of failure only resulted in newer and better things for Munson. His willingness to serve as the Baghdad Bob of Durham in no way kept him from getting a gig with ESPN, where he retains his "expert" status on legal matters despite his decidedly un-expert takes.

Munson did not stand alone in his inability to see well-established innocence. Among the other hindsight-challenged members of the sports media was ESPN's Bomani Jones, who in February 2007 reported from the first Duke lacrosse game since their previous season had been canceled because of the rape charges.

In his discussions with students on campus, Jones spoke with several students who wanted to express their support for the wrongly accused lacrosse players. One kid, Chris Antonacci, sounded (gasp!) just happy the lacrosse team could play a game again: "Around here, we believe the guys [former players Reade Seligmann, Collin Finnerty, and Dave Evans] are innocent," Antonacci said, "and that [last] season should not have been canceled."[26]

Jones pounced on this mere statement of the obvious like a leopard on a gazelle:

> Perhaps that's true, but that's no reason to celebrate the team. After all, none of the three players charged with crimes surrounding a March 9, 2006, house party are still on the team.
>
> While the cancellation of the season may have been premature, plenty came to light when they left the field. Too much to be ignored.[27]

What's this? Too much to be ignored? What kind of twisted, deep-seated evil "came to light" about this lacrosse team?

> The ad hoc committee commissioned by Duke president Richard Brodhead and Academic Council Chair Paul Haagen found that lacrosse players were involved in thirty-six separate disciplinary incidents in the last three academic

years, including destruction of property on campus, public
urination and numerous alcohol-related incidents.[28]

I must confess, I laughed out loud when I read this paragraph.
Seriously? You tried and failed to convict them as rapists, so for your
next act you charge them for acting like college students? How
pathetic. My research assistant (Answers.com) tells me that anywhere
between thirty and thirty-five students play on a college lacrosse team.
For nearly one hundred different individuals between the ages of
eighteen and twenty-two to amass only thirty-six minor incidents of
law-breaking on a college campus over three years is hardly surpris-
ing.

In fact, it's disappointing. When I was nineteen, my technical term
for amassing thirty-six disciplinary violations was "Tuesday." What
Jones was really doing was continuing a smear campaign against college kids for behaving like college kids. The technical term in journalism for this is "grasping at straws."

But Jones wasn't done yet:

Have people forgotten about the claim by Kim Roberts,
one of the dancers hired that evening, that the players
hurled racial slurs at her? Or the report in the *Raleigh
News and Observer* that one partygoer told one of the
dancers to "thank your grandpa for my cotton shirt," an
obvious slavery reference?[29]

Evidence in the record gives proof of a racial slur used by the
lacrosse players. What Jones conveniently leaves out of his account,
however, is that Kim Roberts, one of the two black dancers, "hurled"
the first racial slur.

In an interview with *60 Minutes*, Roberts reveals what exactly happened:

> "I called him a little dick white boy," she recalls laughing. "And how he couldn't get it on his own and had to pay for it. So, he was mad. And it ended with him callin' me the n-word. And it echoed, so you heard n.... once, and then you heard, n...., n...., n...."
>
> Roberts acknowledges *her taunting* [emphasis added] provoked that remark but tells Bradley, "But when I think about it again, I say he could've said black girl. You know what I mean? He could've said black girl. He didn't have to go that route."
>
> A neighbor also told police he overheard a player yelling in Roberts' direction "Thank your grandfather for my cotton shirt."[30]

Roberts is right: the lacrosse player didn't have to go that route, but an honest reporter would have provided the context.

The student that Jones cites in his article makes the point that a few bad apples don't spoil the bunch, saying in reference to the alleged racist slurs, "The whole team shouldn't suffer for the actions of a few."[31]

But predictably, that line of thought does not go very far with Bomani Jones:

> Even if that's true—and it's definitely debatable—the overall body of misbehavior of this team wasn't the reflection of a few people. That track record was built by several players over a span of years—too many sins over too much time to be written off as anything isolated.[32]

Really?! If the legal equivalent of Winston Churchill visited Durham, he would certainly have said, "Never have so many suffered so much for so little." The completely over-the-top effort to paint an entire group of young men as guilty of *something*—racism and sexism, if not rape—highlights nothing less than the obsessions of the liberal media.

As KC Johnson says in *Durham-in-Wonderland*:

> Given Jones' branding the entire lacrosse team as racists because one player uttered a racial slur as part of a racially charged argument, Joan Foster wonders why the espn.com author elected to ignore the findings of the Coleman Committee report on the question of the team's racial attitudes. (After a comprehensive inquiry, the committee discovered no evidence of racist or sexist on-campus behavior.)[33]

In other words, the same ad hoc committee that produced the instances of petty misbehavior that Bomani Jones used to cast an aura of guilt over the Duke lacrosse team reported that the lacrosse team had *no* history of racism or sexism. Committee chairman James Coleman wrote, "We looked closely but found no compelling evidence to support claims that these players are racist or have a record of sexual violence."[34] Wouldn't an honest reporter have made note of that?

Coleman also described team members' drinking habits as "deplorable but pretty typical of what you see with other Duke students who abuse alcohol."

In other words, they were kids—but the sort of kids the liberal media don't like, and so they were dragged through the mud without a second thought to their innocence or to journalistic integrity. That's what you get from the liberal sports media.

CHAPTER NINE

THE NEW RACISM

Everyone loves the NFL playoffs, as teams get winnowed down to play in the ultimate American spectacle, the Super Bowl. And the inherent drama of the games means the sports media are often at their best during the playoffs too—except when they take a relatively inconsequential event and blow it way out of proportion.

On January 19, 2014, only moments after deflecting the NFC championship game–sealing interception into the waiting hands of a friendly linebacker, Seattle Seahawks cornerback Richard Sherman decided to unleash his inner Ric Flair in a postgame interview. Fox Sports' Erin Andrews asked Sherman about the play, and what followed was pure television gold. In a full-throated roar, the likes of which would make the "Nature Boy" himself proud, Sherman—huge, dreadlocked, tattooed, enraged, and black—let loose with a tirade for the ages: "I'm the best corner in the game! When you try me with a sorry receiver like Crabtree, that's the result you gonna get! Don't you ever talk about me. [...] Don't you open your mouth about the best, or I'm gonna shut it for you real quick!"[1]

It was one of the most hilarious things ever to happen on a football field. Well, in my mind it was funny. Apparently I was in the minority, because in a matter of minutes, Twitter exploded with people reacting not only to Sherman's postgame interview, but also to his taunting of 49ers receiver Michael Crabtree and quarterback Colin Kaepernick. Strong words were used—most of them condemning Sherman as a loudmouth and a bad sport.[2]

But the next day, when the media took over the debate, a different word started getting used. That word was "thug." In fact, as reported by *Deadspin*, a group called iQMedia, a company that does media platform research, said that the word "thug" was used 625 times in closed-captioning across all television markets on the day after the Sherman interview aired. The TV broadcast of the Boston-based *Dennis & Callahan Show*, on WEEI, apparently logged twelve "thug" mentions in two minutes alone.[3] Not too shabby.

Why does this matter?

It matters for two reasons.

First, while the word "thug" can be applied to anyone, from the likes of former Patriot tight end Aaron Hernandez to actor Alec Baldwin, according to taste, the media view it as a word that almost always references someone who is black.

The other reason this matters is that when the debate over Richard Sherman happened on Twitter—in other words, among the people at large—"thug" did not get a lot of play. The few racist trolls out there went straight to the N-word. But the racist stuff came from the fringe. Most people upset at Sherman were upset at his behavior, not his skin tone; they disliked his alleged lack of sportsmanship (he received a penalty for taunting on the play); and some didn't like a football player talking like a professional wrestler. But for the American sports media, this was another teaching moment in which they could tell us all just how deeply ignorant and racist they believe the average American to be.

Still, they faced a problem. While the few racist reactions used the N-word with various epithets preceding it, *Sports Center* couldn't air a debate with the caption "Is Richard Sherman a 'No-Class N*****?" They needed some other word to bring the racial debate to the fore, something racially charged but not an overt slur. Sometime between the end of the game on Sunday and the start of the news cycle on Monday, the metaphorical memo went out to all concerned: just as "fiery" can be code for Latinos and "scrappy" can be code for white guys, "thug" can be racist code-speak for black people—at least to the media.

The Monday after the game was the most thuggish day in American media in years, as the American sports media trolled the country trying to spark a debate about why white people feel threatened by black men and are unhappy at seeing them succeed, which was an odd accusation if you consider that the American people had recently elected a black man president of the United States—twice. It was also an odd accusation given that black athletes and coaches are among the most popular in the country.

But the sports media wanted this story because they are obsessed with race and will run with any "racist" story they can get. And they absolutely love racist witch-hunts.

Consider, for instance, the case of Steve Lyons. Lyons, former broadcaster for Fox, was fired immediately after a game during which he made some less-than-great references to Lou Piniella's Hispanic heritage. From the original AP story:

Piniella had made an analogy involving the luck of finding
a wallet, then briefly used a couple of Spanish phrases during Friday's broadcast. Lyons said that Piniella was "habla-
ing Espanol"—butchering the conjugation for the word "to
speak"—and added, "I still can't find my wallet."

"I don't understand him, and I don't want to sit too
close to him now," Lyons continued. Lyons claimed he was
kidding.[4]

Lyons could have saved his breath about "kidding." There was a
time, in the 1960s and 1970s when stewardesses had anatomically
luminescent uniforms and newborn infants were handed a Marlboro
eight seconds after birth, when Lyons's comments would have been
called kidding. Those times are gone. Nowadays, even a hint of a
racially insensitive remark, even if the speaker is kidding, even if the
allegedly racially insensitive remark is about a minority group not
usually categorized as a minority group (Piniella's parents were from
Spain, not from south of the border), can be enough to wreck a career.

In a more egregious error of judgment, San Francisco talk show
host Larry Krueger once referred to the San Francisco Giants lineup
as a bunch of "brain-dead Caribbean hitters."[5] As a result, Krueger
was canned. Now he can take a long vacation (I hear Antigua is lovely
this time of year). Long-time Vikings radioman Lee Hamilton resigned
after being quoted by the *San Diego Union-Tribune* as having said:
"I think it's real hard to find an African American who can come in
and do sports talk across the board and be able to talk about a lot of
different things."[6] Now, you can agree or disagree with this—I happen
to disagree—but this hardly amounts to "Segregation now! Segregation forever!" In fact, the funniest thing about it is that Hamilton
managed to conjoin the politically correct term "African American"

and a dumbo generalization about black sports commentators. That quotation, in addition to Hamilton's calling Hideki Irabu a "fat jap,"[7] was enough to end a pretty nice run as a radio broadcaster.

Look outside the sports world: Michael Richards is no longer the universally loved goofball named Kramer on *Seinfeld*. He is now a universally unemployable pariah after launching into an inexplicably awful tirade at a heckler in an LA comedy club. Meanwhile, black sportscasters like Michael Irvin can make absurd charges of pre–Civil War–era crossbreeding, and there's no backlash whatsoever. On the *Dan Patrick Show*, Irvin attempted to explain how the Cowboys' white quarterback Tony Romo was so athletic. You'll get a good laugh from his hypothesis if you're an idiot, or Michael Wilbon, or both: "[Romo's] great, great, great, great Grandma pulled one of them studs up outta the barn."[8]

Do me a favor, just for one moment, and imagine if a white broadcaster on a radio show, discussing a very intelligent black athlete like, say, Richard Sherman, had explained away Sherman's considerable intelligence as the result of his great-great-great-great-grandma having had sex with a plantation owner. He would have been fired— and not just from his job: the network would have loaded him into a cannon and fired him into a lake of fire. There would be national outrage. Yet Michael Irvin continues to be employed by a radio station and the NFL Network.

The point is that racism is punished in our society today. Well, unless the racist in question is black, in which case you get a free pass and perhaps a multiyear, six- or even seven-figure contract from a major sports network. But there is no institutional racism in this country against "people of color." That is long gone. In fact, many institutions—including the NFL with its "Rooney Rule" requiring teams to interview minority candidates for coaching and management positions—go out of their way to increase their "diversity." And "racism" is one of the worst charges that can be made against anyone in the court of public opinion. No one—by which I mean maybe 1 percent of the American people—is "for" racism. Everyone—by which I mean about 99 percent of the American people—is against it. That doesn't mean that racism has completely disappeared in our society or that the racist acts aren't still committed—but they shock us now because they are so rare and universally regarded as wrong. Comedian Tom Shillue sums up the current state of race relations in America perfectly: "The only people hurt by racism these days are the racists."[9]

Real victims of racism these days are few, so, by necessity, the liberal media, wanting to relive their glory days of the civil rights era, must invent them, and that is the function of the New Racism—namely, finding racism where there isn't any.

Which speaks to the point: racism is no longer a social institution, like Jim Crow, that needs to be abolished. It's a business worth millions of dollars to shysters like Jesse Jackson and Al Sharpton who shake down corporations for payoffs; and it is worth a ton in ratings and notoriety for sports media racial hucksters like ESPN's Michael Wilbon who inject their vile hate-venom into every topic that they conceivably can. And even some that they conceivably can't. On *Pardon the Interruption*, Tony Kornheiser and Michael Wilbon discussed comments made by well-known University of Texas booster Red McCombs about the hiring process that led to UT picking Charlie Strong (who is black) to succeed Mack Brown (who is white) as UT's next head football coach. Red McCombs was highly displeased with the hire and let fly while on the air with an ESPN affiliate in San Antonio: "I think the whole thing is a bit sideways.... I don't have any doubt that Charlie is a fine coach. I think he would make a great position coach, maybe a coordinator. But I don't believe [he belongs at] what should be one of the three most powerful university programs in the world right now at UT-Austin. I don't think it adds up."[10]

McCombs went on:

> I think it is a kick in the face. Beyond the fact of what actually happened. We have boosters that have a lot of knowledge about the game. When we decided to go get Mack—from the time we decided to go get Mack to about 30 hours later to have a press conference here and it was done—we had a lot of input before we went after him.
>
> So I don't know what the big rush was. I was kind of pleased that [Texas athletic director Steve] Patterson already said that he'd like to get it done in the middle of January. That seemed logical to me. I'm a team player, but I think they went about it wrong and made the selection wrong.[11]

Now, to be clear, McCombs's comment that Strong might only be good enough for a position coach at UT is beyond insane. Strong was 23 and 3 as the head coach at Louisville. The coaching position he was most suited for was head coach. But plenty of people (myself included) thought Charlie Strong might be in over his head at Texas. Strong was notorious at Louisville for hating the "political" side of the job: doing media, selling the program, hanging out with rich donors. The head-coaching job at Texas, at least under Mack Brown, was as much political as it was about football: schmoozing with millionaire donors and kissing the ring (and if necessary, the behind) of the guy who's buying you the new wing of the "student-athlete" center.

None of those people, and certainly not Red McCombs, ever stood against hiring Strong because he was black. In fact, Red McCombs is the cofounder of the San Antonio Spurs, which, if you haven't noticed, employs a higher percentage of black men than most businesses and more than have ever been employed by Michael Wilbon. But of course that's exactly the well-worn path that Michael Wilbon wanted to take us down on *Pardon the Interruption*. Wilbon called UT's new (as of November 2013) athletic director Steve Patterson more "progressive"[12] (read: less racist) than most, having come from a college basketball background as opposed to a football background.

Wilbon's not-so-subtle message was that football, especially Southern college football, remains—against all evidence to the contrary, including black coaches, like Charlie Strong at Louisville—a bastion of, in leftist speak, white male privilege. But Wilbon didn't stop there; he then warned of the great obstacles and hurdles that Charlie Strong would have to overcome at Texas. Specifically, the "good old boy network" (read: angry, racist, white Republicans) that rule the roost there. So here you have the University of Texas, the largest school in the state and the wealthiest athletic department in the country, hiring the first black head coach in school history, and Wilbon wants us to fear the "good old boy network"?

Quick question: How entrenched and all-powerful could this alleged network of racist good old boys be if they couldn't succeed in stopping the appointment of a "progressive" athletic director or the hiring of a black head football coach? In fact, let's go a step further, because the University of Texas is not the only school in the Lone Star State to hire a black head coach. Texas A&M, UT's archrival, and the second-biggest program in the state, actually beat the "progressives" in Austin to the punch when they hired Kevin Sumlin (who is black) in December 2011. So here you have the Great State of Texas, the western anchor of the Deep South; here in this supposed cauldron of fiery racial hate, the two largest schools in the state have hired black head coaches, and to Michael Wilbon the real story is the power of the "good old boy network." *Really?*

It wasn't so long ago that Wilbon and others were lamenting...check that...screaming at the top of their lungs about how there weren't more than four black head coaches in all of the top 120 schools in college football. Here you have two black head coaches at the two biggest institutions in arguably the biggest football state in the country, and the story is that Texas is racist? This is the "New Racism" at work. Wilbon can't let us sit back and take stock of what should be an awesome moment in race and sports and applaud how these hires show just how far we've come, because then people might...you know...realize how far we've come.

Nor has Wilbon confined his hysterical bleating to *Pardon the Interruption* or coaching moves. In 2010, when the Redskins were in the midst of year seventeen of their rebuilding program, head coach Mike Shanahan (who is white) pulled quarterback Donovan McNabb (who is black) from a football game in the final two minutes and put in white quarterback Rex Grossman. Shanahan explained his decision this way: "I felt with the time, with no timeouts, Rex gave us the best chance to win in that scenario. Everything is sped up when you don't have timeouts. It's got to be automatic. People forget how quick things are in that two minutes. It's like learning a new language. Are you asking me if we played poorly? Yes, we did."[13]

Jason Reid of the *Washington Post* offered further explanation for the coach's decision: "Redskins Coach Mike Shanahan said Monday that Donovan McNabb's lingering injuries played a role in the coach's decision to bench his starting quarterback Sunday.... McNabb wasn't able to fully practice and Shanahan said that from a 'cardio-vascular standpoint,' McNabb couldn't handle the fast-paced two-minute offense."[14]

That knowing-the-offense, being-in-shape, giving-your-team-the-best-chance-to-win mumbo-jumbo wouldn't fly for Michael Wilbon, who wrote this in the *Washington Post*:

> Look, I've long ago declared my bias toward McNabb and I'm not going to spin away from it now. McNabb, though, hasn't played all that well and has said so. He wasn't par-ticularly effective Sunday in Detroit, either. And indications are now that the Shanahans, father and son, don't much like the way McNabb prepares for games. Mike's assertion makes it sound like McNabb is some dummy, an ominous characterization he'd better be careful about, lest he run into some cultural trouble in greater Washington, D.C.[15]

Pretty funny that Wilbon feels comfortable enough threatening the cultural wrath of "greater Washington, D.C.," after taking one of his highly publicized large-scale bowel movements on the city, call-ing it a "terrible" sports town. He wrote that despite living in D.C. for thirty-two years, he "barely call[s] it home." Apparently Wilbon isn't worried about incurring any "cultural trouble in greater Wash-ington, D.C.," himself. What Wilbon did here was take a meaningless quarterback change by a lousy team (I say that as a native Washing-tonian and lifelong fan) in a lousy game, and elevate it to Rodney King–like proportions. Conveniently forgotten in all this was that Shanahan, as head coach, was involved in the Redskins' decision to trade for Donovan McNabb in Shanahan's first season with the team. He, apparently, saw a serviceable starting quarterback in the aging veteran. I, on the other hand, when I looked at Donovan McNabb, thought of soup: not the stringy chicken stuff they send in aid packages to kids in Eastern Europe, but the thick, industrial-strength stuff that you have to wear elastic-waist sweatpants to eat and that McNabb advertised for Campbell's Chunky brand. Clearly, though, Wilbon saw Rosa Parks in pads and cleats.

Again, the New Racism's "heroes" aren't actual heroes; they're millionaires who get pulled from the two-minute drill. But look at the precedent set here: because McNabb was out of shape, past his prime, and unable to understand the offense (after his stint with the Redskins, he failed in Minnesota, "despite," as race-crazed liberal sports reporters might add, having a black head coach there), Wilbon turned Shanahan's concerns over McNabb's football IQ into a referendum on black people as a whole, or at least those who live in D.C.

John Feinstein was not to be outdone by Wilbon. After ESPN's Chris Mortensen reported that Mike Shanahan had to drastically cut down the size of his playbook in order for McNabb to learn it (and even then, with the CliffsNotes version of the playbook, McNabb still had trouble calling the right plays in the huddle), Feinstein went off:

> Then I saw Mortensen's "report." That's when I went on Washington Post Live and accused Shanahan of racial coding because I believe if he was Mortensen's source that is absolutely what he was doing. And if it was, Shanahan is a despicable human being and, yes, I think he's using racial coding and yes I think he should be fired. If anyone wants to disagree with me about that, fine....[16]

Basically Wilbon and Feinstein are claiming that this info about McNabb's not knowing the playbook and being out of shape never would have been leaked to the media if McNabb were white. As if information questioning a quarterback's IQ is somehow kept secret if the quarterback is white (somewhere Tim Tebow is calling BS on this). I have a different theory though. Maybe, just maybe, after getting accused of racism at every turn by an unhinged and race-obsessed liberal sports media, Shanahan released that information believing (naïvely) it would show he made the move for football reasons. Maybe he released it thinking that everyone would see that he didn't really harbor racial animus toward the quarterback he traded a second-round pick for, and that in reality McNabb was an overweight, over-the-hill, in-over-his-head player who was past his prime. It's too cute that Mike Shanahan might have thought that the releasing of facts would dissuade the D.C. sports media from labeling him a racist. It's so cute I just want to poke him in the nose. Boop!

But whatever his motivations for releasing the information, the sports media's handling of said information was beyond ridiculous, though that's not totally unexpected from a group of race-peddlers, especially in Washington, D.C. Other aspects of the sports media's desire to preserve racism and racist lingo, no matter the cost, have proved far more troubling.

To my knowledge, there is only one word in the English language that dramatically switches meaning based on who speaks it. A car is always a car, a potato is always a potato, and a marsupial is always a marsupial. But the New Racism has furnished us with a word that forms and shape-shifts like Mystique on meth. And that word is the N-word. Ironically, the word that true heroes and civil rights leaders of yore probably wanted done away with more than any other word in the English language, regardless of who said it, has now been safely ensconced in the American lexicon for the foreseeable future—*but only when it's said by black people*. For it is a sad but true fact that one of the negative legacies of the civil rights movement in this country was that it stole the N-word away from white people (a good thing) and made it the exclusive province of black people (a not-so-good thing). The end result is that when the N-word is used by white people, it means cotton fields, whip-lashings, fire hoses, German shepherds, and Jim Crow. But when it's used by black people, it means rainbows, butterflies, unicorns, and fuzzy bunny slippers.

Nothing brought this galactically hypocritical garbage to light more than when an overly intoxicated Philadelphia Eagles wide receiver named Riley Cooper got caught dropping N-bombs by a camera phone at a Kenny Chesney concert: "I will jump that fence and fight every n***** here, bro."[17]

Yes, I am appalled too. How a man who sings about strawberry wine and going to restaurants barefoot could cause such an explosion of racial hatred is beyond me. But as for what Riley Cooper actually said, let's go through some facts. Cooper is an idiot and wrong for doing what he did. But he never acted on his threat. He never jumped the fence and fought anybody. For all intents and purposes, it was an ignorant lapse of judgment while drunk (as opposed to Bob Costas's ignorant lapses in judgment, which occur while he's stone-cold sober), and it appeared to be an isolated incident, since nobody on the Eagles roster recalled Cooper using that word before or showing any sign of racial hostility.

The Eagles fined Cooper, made him publicly apologize for his comments, and then sent him out for sensitivity training. But that wasn't good enough for the sports media's racial flash mob. In fact, it wasn't just the sports media. Michael A. Nutter, the mayor of Philadelphia, took precious time away from running Philly's public school system into the ground to get on his soapbox and push for stronger action against Cooper: "In a year when we celebrated the great achievements of Jackie Robinson in the movie *42*, it is truly saddening that racial epithets are still being hurled like baseballs, or by a football player, at the human dignity of African-Americans and others. This incident is a disgrace, and cannot be excused by just paying a fine, as if it were a parking ticket."[18]

Don't worry, Mr. Mayor: as someone who has spent years in the locker rooms of professional sports teams, I can assure you that racial epithets are "hurled like baseballs" by black players far more than they are by white players. Nutter even went on to lay out exactly how the Eagles could fire Riley Cooper for what he said:

> As the Mayor of this City and an African-American man, I find the remarks made by Riley Cooper repugnant, insensitive and ignorant, and all of us, regardless of race or nationality, should be offended by these comments. I recognize that the private sector is very different than the public sector in terms of rules and procedures, but I would note that in our government, if an executive branch "at-will" employee, somewhat similar to Mr. Cooper's status with the Eagles, made such comments, I would insist on a suspension at a minimum and would seriously have to evaluate terminating such an individual from employment with the City.[19]

Michael Wilbon and Dan Patrick, though sports reporters who are supposed to know something about the sports they report, rebuked NFL commissioner Roger Goodell for not doing something he has no power to do: impose an NFL punishment on Cooper. These sorts of disciplinary decisions are left, by the NFL's collecting bargaining agreement, to the teams themselves to decide. But of course that's no reason for reporters like Wilbon and Patrick not to grandstand, especially when the issue is race.

Sometimes you have to wonder about the real-world experience of these sports reporters. It's not exactly a secret that the N-word gets tossed around NFL locker rooms like a dirty jock strap, albeit by black players. Yet nothing is ever said by the media—not by Dan Patrick, not by Michael Wilbon, and not by big-city mayors. Yet it was in this case. Why? Not because of the N-word itself, but because of who said it. Riley Cooper's crime wasn't using the N-word; it was that he was white. Is that progress?

What was even more convoluted than the sports media's reaction to Riley Cooper was the reaction of some of his teammates. Running back LeSean McCoy wasn't quite so ready to welcome Cooper back with open arms. According to CSNPhilly's Geoff Mosher: "'Ain't nothing to prove. He said how he felt,' McCoy said. 'He's still a teammate. I'm still going to block for him. I'm still gonna show great effort. Just on a friendship level, and as a person, I can't really respect somebody like that. I think as a team, we need to move past it. There are some things that are going to be hard to work with, to be honest.'"[20]

Really? That's odd, because McCoy showed no such moral hangups about showing "respect" for fellow teammate Michael Vick, who had brutally tortured and slaughtered hundreds of defenseless dogs for sport.

Now, to their credit, most of the Eagles don't live in McCoyville. DeSean Jackson, Jason Avant, DeMeco Ryans, and even Michael Vick himself were all able to publicly embrace Cooper and welcome him back to the team without any apparent issues. But McCoy wasn't alone in his moral back-assward-ness. Back in 2009, when Michael Vick was trying to reenter the league, Michael Wilbon wrote the journalistic equivalent of a love letter to Eagles owner Jeffrey Lurie in the *Washington Post*. Wilbon called Lurie's signing of Vick after his stint in the federal pen for dog-killing "the most difficult decision in his professional life," and wrote that Lurie had always "seemed to me to be one of the most thoughtful owners in sports."[21]

Lurie was clearly, in Wilbon's words, "conflicted if not outright tortured by the decision, which was playing much better nationally than in Philly."[22] There were other owners who might have wanted to sign Vick but, according to Wilbon, those other owners "didn't have the fortitude to make the call that Lurie did."[23] To say that Wilbon is laying it on thick here is an understatement. What he's doing is turning Eagles owner Jeffrey Lurie into a hero. Jeffrey Lurie, conflicted from within and persecuted from without by petty, small-minded simpletons who . . . you know . . . don't want to see dog-electrocuters get multimillion-dollar contracts, is an army of one against a nation of seething intolerance. Lurie rose to the occasion and made a decision that no one else had the guts to make.

Please. Yes, there were some PETA protesters at Vick's court hearings and there may have been the odd bearded "Fur Is Evil" hipster sipping a macchiato outside of Eagles practice, but it took no great courage to sign Michael Vick. Though there was no hotter topic on sports talk radio at the time, there were just as many hosts and callers in favor of Michael Vick's getting a second chance (I was one of them) as there were demanding he be fed to the dogs. So the idea that Lurie was some kind of "hero" in all of this is absurd. But the point here is not Jeffrey Lurie, it's what gets people in the New Racism ginned up, and whom they come after and why. Here's Wilbon heaping praise on an owner for taking a chance on a dog killer while at the same time ferociously attacking NFL commissioner Roger Goodell for not coming down harder on Riley Cooper.[24] Priorities? In what kind of whacked-out, crazy world is Michael Vick less repulsive and less in need of forgiveness and mercy than Riley Cooper? In the world of the New Racism, that's where.

And does anyone really believe that LeSean McCoy loses respect for every *black* player on his team who uses the N-word? On the flip side, is there anyone who thinks Michael Wilbon would have written an article praising the courage and fortitude of Jeffrey Lurie if Michael Vick had been white? Of course not. Again, in the New Racism, the crime is not the slur being used but the skin color of the person who uses it. Michael Wilbon doesn't care any more about those dogs than he cares about the N-word (which, as we will see shortly, he says proudly on an almost daily basis). He cares about the identity of who said it and whether that person fits in his New Racism good-old-boy club.

No story illustrated this more than the Jonathan Martin/Richie Incognito fiasco of 2013. This is a really weird one, folks, so bear with me. In late October 2013, Dolphins tackle Jonathan Martin suddenly left the team, saying he needed to address "emotional issues."[25] For anyone doubting the success of the political correctness/wussification-of-America movement in this country, read that line again: a 6-foot, 5-inch, 320-pound offensive tackle left an NFL football team to deal with "emotional issues." I rest my case.

A week later, the Dolphins suspended fellow offensive lineman Richie Incognito after it allegedly became apparent that the "emotional issues" stemmed from Incognito's bullying of Martin. Martin's camp made public a voice message in which Incognito had referred to Martin (who is half-white and half-black) as a "half-n***** piece of shit."[26] Incognito then went on to say that he was going to go after Martin's family, saying, "I'm going to slap your real mother across the face."[27] Then, as if this Taster's Choice moment between bros couldn't get any more heartfelt, Incognito capped it off with this great term of friendly endearment, "I want to shit in your fucking mouth."[28] (Side note: It was awful nice of Incognito to offer to do that for free. I hear there's a guy in lower Manhattan who charges $500 for that.)

At this point, however much a digression it might seem, I'd like to make my case for bringing back the military draft. Or at least bringing it back for members of the media. Because here's where having a sports media with more guys who have spent some time in the military, or a police department, or a fire department would have been helpful. As someone who has spent time in two of the three above services (U.S. Army and FDNY), I've had several of these kinds of relationships. I had a black friend in the army who told me he was going to beat the "oppressor" out of me and do odd things to my skull after I was dead. I then told him I was going to displace him and his whole family like an unwanted band of Brazilian rainforest dwellers. I had a Puerto Rican friend in the fire department who told me to make sure I didn't come to work sick, because then I would be poisoning him the same way my ancestors had poisoned his people by bringing diseases over from Europe. I then made a joke that I can't share with you because the racial rules are different for me than they are for him. But the point is he laughed. The bigger point is that I would have put my life on the line for him, and he would have done the same for me; same thing with my friend in the army.

Back and forth it would go, and, especially in the army, all of it occurred over a lot of beers and more than a few laughs. The reality is that in jobs and professions where you get your hands dirty, there's a different code of etiquette. It's an untaught, unwritten, yet mutually understood language rooted in filth, violence, sexual perversion, and racial angst that borders on the insane to anyone on the outside looking or listening in, yet one that preserves some sense of sanity and balance in a world that has very little sanity and balance. It's that way in the military, the police department, and the fire department, and evidently it's that way in the NFL as well. It's the secret language of men. But it might as well be Swahili to our sports media, the vast majority of whom have never held a job like that. Not that I'm blaming them for it; if you went straight to college and straight from college to a career, good for you. God bless. But part of the job of being in the media is to at least attempt to understand the world and the people that you're reporting on, not to try and judge it based solely on what makes sense to you in your own worldview. But this is precisely what the leftist sports media do.

It took me all of three minutes after listening to the voice messages that Incognito had left for Martin to realize that, although it had obviously gone very wrong for some reason at some point, there was a relationship between Incognito and Martin. They were friends. It took the racial flash mob in the sports media all of three minutes to try and turn this into a referendum on bullying and racial politics. They began asking how we can change the culture of NFL locker rooms and calling for the ousting or suspending of virtually every coach and executive in Miami. The flash mob had a problem though. Jonathan Martin was a terrible "victim." At first he didn't speak at all. Then when he did, his few public statements were confusing and not specific. The pre-draft reports about Martin's being "sensitive" started coming out as well, which was a major reason why a lot of teams passed on him.

Then Richie Incognito started releasing his own text messages from his correspondence with Martin, over a thousand of them, including one where Martin said he was going to send someone over to Incognito's house to rape him with "sandpaper condoms"[29] and ejaculate on his face (in the language of men, this is how we say "Hello"). The messages Incognito released proved even more that if there was "abuse" or "bullying" going on here, it was a two-way street. Then another funny thing happened: the "barbarians" fought back. The NFL players who shared the same locker room, and the same unwritten language of men that Martin and Incognito had shared, started fighting back against the sports media's attempts to intrude upon and radically alter a world they had no business trying to change.

Former Dolphin Lydon Murtha, who played with both Incognito and Martin, wrote a piece on the Monday Morning Quarterback page of SI.com that fully explained why Incognito had invested so much time in Martin and why their relationship was as complex as it was. According to Murtha, Martin was very "standoffish" when he first joined the team, and as a team leader, Incognito was tasked with bringing Martin "out of his shell." But, according to Murtha, bringing Martin out of his shell was no easy task:

> That's where Incognito ran into a problem. Personally, I know when a guy can't handle razzing. You can tell that some guys just aren't built for it. Incognito doesn't have that filter. He was the jokester on the team, and he joked with everybody from players to coaches. That voicemail he sent came from a place of humor, but where he really screwed up was using the N-word. That, I cannot condone, and it's probably the biggest reason he's not with the team right now. *Odd thing is, I've heard Incognito call Martin the same thing to his face in meetings and all Martin did was laugh* [emphasis added]. Many more worse things were said about others in the room from all different parties. It's an Animal House. Now Incognito's being slandered as a racist and a bigot, and unfortunately that's never going to

be wiped clean because of all the wrong he's done people in his past. But if you really know who Richie is, he's a really good, kind man and far from a racist.[30]

This article should have been written by a member of the sports media. But no member of the sports media was interested in digging deeper to find out the truth of the relationship between Incognito and Martin, because as soon as the N-bomb was dropped, the liberal sports media had the story they wanted. Black players, incidentally, seemed just as offended by Jonathan Martin for not sticking up for himself as they were by anything Incognito said. On WFAN in New York, the Giants' Antrel Rolle let fly at Martin: "Was Richie Incognito wrong? Absolutely. But I think the other guy is just as much to blame as Richie, because he allowed it to happen. At this level, you're a man. You're not a little boy. You're not a freshman in college. You're a man."[31]

It's an unwritten rule that in order for the media to truly make someone a victim, that person has to be a sympathetic figure—someone you not only identify with, but feel sorry for. Thanks to Richie Incognito's lawyers and players like Lydon Murtha (who were the only people who did any real reporting on this story), the sports media had a very hard time turning Jonathan Martin into a "victim" and instead left him looking like a weak, confused wimp who might have been partly culpable for the over-the-top razzing by Incognito. So instead the media shifted to talking about the toxic culture of the Dolphins locker room in particular and NFL locker rooms in general, which was just as well for their storyline about the need for progressive reform of an overly manly sport.

In November 2013, the N-word came up again, this time in basketball after a scuffle on the court involving the Clippers and the

Thunder. Clippers forward Matt Barnes, who was ejected during the fight, shared a few thoughts on Twitter: "I love my teammates like family, but I'm DONE standing up for these n[******]! All this shit does is cost me money,"[32] Barnes wrote before deleting the tweet.

Instead of sparking universal outrage and condemnation from the sports media (as it would if a white player had tweeted this), the tweet made the flash mob decide that this would be an awesome time to debate who can use the N-word. On *Inside the NBA* on TNT, Charles Barkley laid out the case:

> I'm a black man. I use the N-word. I'm going to continue to use the N-word with my black friends, with my white friends. They are my friends. What I do with my black friends is not up to white America to dictate to me what's appropriate and inappropriate. What we say in the locker room, the language we use sometime it's homophobic, sometime it's sexist, and a lot of times it's racist. White America don't get to dictate how me and Shaq talk to each other. And they have been trying to infiltrate themselves saying, "Well, you guys use it. It's in rap music." No, no, no, no, no. That's not the same.[33]

Um, actually it is. Barkley can tell himself whatever he wants. But the word means the same thing no matter who says it. And Barnes didn't confine his use of the N-word to the locker room. He tweeted it out in public. Had he used it in the locker room only, as he and his teammates probably do ninety-seven times a day, nobody would have reported it. But there's a bigger point to be made here: Who exactly are these white people who are trying to "infiltrate themselves"? Riley Cooper was denounced by white people every bit as much, if not more, than he was by black people. Even Richie Incognito's friend Lydon Murtha (who is white) said he shouldn't have used that word. Who are all these white people out there who are just *dying* to use the N-word? It just seems like there are, because the media only report it when white people use the N-word. The other eleventy billion times the word gets used, it's used by minorities, and normally to great financial benefit by said minorities.

Lil Wayne, who had the gall to criticize Riley Cooper on Twitter,[34] can hardly utter three words in any of his songs without dropping an N-bomb, and he's made himself a millionaire while doing it. If the media were to report every time a black person said the N-word, we would need an N-word channel.

Barkley wasn't alone in his take on who had exclusive rights on the N-word. Also on *Inside the NBA*, Shaquille O'Neal weighed in: "Chuck makes a good point. In the Ebonic culture we have programmed ourselves to use the word positive. We have G14 classification to say it to each other. But when we say it to each other, believe it or not, it's in the positive sense."[35]

I call BS on this as well. There are plenty of derogatory uses of the N-word among black people, especially when someone uses the word "house" before it. I watched two guys in the army get in a knockdown, drag-out fight after one guy called the other that particular name. They would definitely have disagreed with Shaq on that one. But again, Shaq's point is consistent with the New Racist mantra: When one black guy calls another black guy the N-word, it means gin blossoms and show ponies. When a white guy does it, it means a barracuda armed with a machete and herpes. The worst part about all this is that this debate took place on an NBA show that was carrying a live game. Can you imagine tuning in trying to watch a game and having to sit through this?

At least Michael Wilbon had the decency to handle his indecency on an actual opinion show. After *Pardon the Interruption* cohost Tony Kornheiser asked Wilbon about Barnes's public use of the N-word, the leader of the racial flash mob went full monty: "People can be upset with me if they want; I, like a whole lot of people, use the N-word all day, every day, my whole life."[36]

Hit the brakes for a second. Follow me on a short trip back to Normalsville, a nice place where things make sense, Russell Brand does not exist, and we don't tolerate bullshit political correctness. Can you imagine if a white broadcaster for ESPN, or any other major sports network, had gotten up there and freely admitted to using the N-word "all day, every day" of his "whole life"? This is a word that is deemed so offensive by Wilbon's employer, among others, that they won't even print it anymore. It gets the same letter followed by dash, dash, dash, treatment that the F-word and countless other expletives have gotten for decades. And here's Wilbon, freely, check that, *proudly* boasting to have used the word every day for his whole life, with no fear of retribution whatsoever—practically daring ESPN to do something about it. That is breathtaking. Even Kornheiser seemed taken aback by Wilbon's brashness, asking Wilbon if NBA commissioner David Stern (who is white) needed to step in and ban players from publicly using the N-word. Wilbon bristled: "I have a problem with—and excuse me, here—white people framing the discussion for the use of the N-word. They better not sit there like plantation owners and tell black people how to use the language that was forced on us!"[37]

And boom goes the dynamite. This is what passes for "sports" coverage in the sports media during the age of the New Racism: a highly paid "analyst" making an analogy between a liberal, Jewish commissioner and a Southern plantation owner, and a league of

millionaire black players and slaves. But look at the shift in direction
from when Riley Cooper used the N-word to when Matt Barnes did.
When Riley Cooper said it, Wilbon was enraged at NFL commissioner Roger Goodell for not dropping the hammer on Cooper:

> I think what is becoming to me a bigger story and more
> important story and a sadder story is Roger Goodell and
> his lightweight reaction to this. This is a chance for the
> Commissioner who likes to use the bully pulpit to just sorta
> smack people around the head...[and] threaten to suspend
> people. "I'm a tough guy. I'm a law and order Commis-
> sioner." He's a lightweight. I am beyond disappointed in
> Roger Goodell. I am angry at Roger Goodell because Roger
> Goodell is a smart man. I covered the NFL for a while. I
> got to know Roger on his way up. And for Roger Goodell
> to hide behind procedure is so lame, it's unspeakably
> lame....
>
> The league has to take action. You're the CEO of the
> NFL. And you like to remind everybody of that. You're bad
> bad Leroy Brown. You like to wear it on people's noses
> publicly. And when the time comes, when something hap-
> pens like this and your league is 70 percent black and you
> don't understand that people are *angry*.... I'm much
> angrier at Roger Goodell than I am at Riley Cooper....
> [Cooper] is in the process of getting it, and he's going to
> have to live with the consequences. Roger Goodell is a
> grown man and just sort of hides behind "well the team
> handles this." *Please*! That is just so borderline just gutless.
> It is unspeakable to me what he has done.[38]

But when Matt Barnes (a black guy) says the very same word, Wilbon gets on a different high horse and proclaims: "They better not sit there like plantation owners and tell black people how to use the language that was forced on us!"

Unreal. While in the thick of the Riley Cooper episode, I was debating with a black caller who couldn't understand why I was so passionate about making the point that it wasn't okay for either white *or black* people to use the N-word. Why did I care so much? he asked. I don't know. Maybe as a talk show host I believe in the power of words. Maybe I believe that if somebody gets called a demeaning word "all day, every day" then sooner or later they start to believe it. Maybe I grew up in a city that was majority black and crime-ridden and I think that word has something to do with the cultural rot and moral decay that you find in so many inner-city neighborhoods.

Here's what I know: the history of slavery is a sad and ugly one, but it's not a uniquely American history, and the history of slavery is not a uniquely black one either. Before Christianity, slavery was pretty much universal, east and west, north and south. In the ancient world, Egyptians kept Jews as slaves, the Greeks kept slaves, the Romans kept slaves, the Persians and Gauls kept slaves. Everyone did until slavery was essentially abolished in Christian Europe during the Middle Ages. The slave trade to the New World colonies came later, but even then, Africans practiced slavery, the Indians of the New World practiced slavery, and more than a million white, Christian Europeans were enslaved by Muslims.

Given all that history, think about this: How many Jews call themselves whatever Pharaoh's thugs used to call them? How many people even remember if their Greek or French ancestors were slaves? How many white, Christian Europeans call themselves kaffirs or infidels or any of the other names that their Islamic slave masters used? The answer is none. Point being, if those cultures could rise above and cast aside the hate language they were subjected to, why can't black people? Why is it so important to keep the N-word? So Lil Wayne can sell records? So Michael Wilbon doesn't have to expand his vocabulary? Sorry, I realize it's a crime under the rule of the New Racism to care more about the self-worth and future of black kids than about Russell Simmons's bank account, but I do. Guilty as charged.

White people aren't angry with black people for using the N-word because they want to use it or because they want to be like "plantation owners" telling black people how "to use language that was forced" on them. It's the polar opposite of that. White people are angry because they naïvely believed we were all fighting for the same thing, which was banishing slurs like that entirely, no matter who said it, only to rather rudely be made aware that they were wrong. Instead, it turns out that what we were fighting for was the New Racism, the permanent preservation of a race-mongering industry, dedicated to making whites feel perpetual guilt and self-loathing while blacks are made to feel like perpetual victims. As sportswriter Mike Wise, a lone voice of reason in this debate, wrote in the *Washington Post* after Wilbon's hideous *Pardon the Interruption* performance: "When you think you're fighting for a less hostile, less confusing and more mutually respectful country for our children to live in and then you find out your idea of a shared purpose wasn't shared by people you like and respect, a real hopelessness sets in."[39]

It's the New Racism that is the factory of that hopelessness. Whether it's in the music industry that benefits tremendously from the use of slurs or the sports entertainment industry that craves race controversies for ratings, "racism" has become a business that peddles denigration as its stock and trade, and the sports media are among its largest franchises. Responding to Wilbon's statement that he had a problem with "white people framing the discussion for the use of the N-word," Wise wrote, "And I have a problem with anyone of any ethnicity telling me that my values and beliefs about eradicating slurs from public and private conversation are less important than having agency over them for personal use—no matter who it hurts, including millions of African Americans who want the word abolished and should have just as much say."[40]

Amen. I am a free man, and you are a free man or woman, made so by the blood, sweat, and tears of men black and white who fought to end slavery in the Civil War and by men and women who fought to end segregation, and whose sacrifice absolved us of the guilt that accompanied both. I won't dishonor them and what they fought and died for by living my life in perpetual guilt over crimes that had nothing to do with me. Nor should any black person live as though he or she is an eternal victim of slavery, which was abolished a hundred and fifty years ago, or of segregation, which was torn down fifty years ago.

We should all be students of history, but not prisoners of it. Time has a funny way of moving on, and so should we. We should learn the lessons of history, one of which is *not* to refight the wars, hatreds, and blood feuds of yore. Yet that's the biggest crime of the New Racism: not just the dishonoring of the memories of those brave souls who fought for freedom in the past, but the depriving of generations of current kids from the true sense of freedom so dearly bought that is their birthright.

AFTERWORD

Can anything be done about the liberal bias and politicization of sports media?

The short answer is yes.

But we need to be realistic. We're never going to get rid of ESPN, no matter how biased or obnoxious it gets. Just as the new media never did away with the mainstream media, we're never going to get rid of the dominant liberal sports media; they're simply too well entrenched.

But what we can do, as with this book, is highlight the failures and bias of the liberal sports media, erode their position of authority, and provide millions of underserved sports fans with real, honest sports reporting.

According to a Gallup poll from the summer of 2014, only 18 percent of the American public has "confidence" in the news they get from television. That's down from 46 percent in 1993. Truth-tellers like former CBS newsman Bernard Goldberg, author of the influential bestseller *Bias*, helped expose the truth about the liberal media. Entrepreneurs, many of them on the political Right, have set up alternatives to the mainstream liberal media. These alternatives, like Fox News, try to provide better, "fair and balanced" reporting, including coverage of stories that the liberal media try to ignore.

That same thing can happen, on a smaller scale, with the sports media. Conservative and nonpolitical sports fans want to be able to talk about the teams they love without having their worldview besmirched and denigrated by a bunch of wannabe Chis Matthewses and Rachel Maddows. Breitbart.com has already launched a great sports website that is not only doing great reporting and analysis on sports but confronting left-wing mainstream sports media bias every day. Conservatives are natural sports fans, because they love competition, revel in American traditions and history (including sports), and appreciate individual hard work and striving for greatness. The demand from conservative sports fans for real sports coverage, liberated from leftist agendas and politically correct spin, is palpable and growing.

The sports world has become politicized, and there's probably nothing that can undo that. Now that the sanctity of our once pristine and unviolated sports sanctum has been breached, our responsibility is to do something about it. It's not something that you or I, in our innocence, signed up to do. But if we want real sports reporting and commentary that's accurate and fair, if we want to thwart an arrogant liberal media that want to remake sports, our country, and ourselves, then we need to shut off the bad guys and tune into the good guys.

With the decisions that you and I make, a better sports media can start today.

ACKNOWLEDGMENTS

Years ago I asked God to give me at least one guide, at least one great friend, at least one confidant, at least one rock that I could lean on, and at least one great love. What I didn't know is that He would combine them all in the same person, my wife, Lara.

As for our son Mitchell, you're the greatest thing I've ever seen. You've single-handedly restored my hope for the world by representing everything that is good about it. Your presence here is living proof that this place is still worth fighting for, and fight I will.

The list of those deserving acknowledgment is far too long, but here's a condensed version: Daniel Flynn for going out of his way to help and advise on this project and others; the awesome editing duo of Harry Crocker and Katharine Spence for making my ranting sound eloquent; Norma and Don Abrams for substitute parenting and support; and Michael Mayhew for being a great patriot and a great friend.

Also, special thanks to the program directors I've had the pleasure of working with and for, especially Bryan Erickson and Craig Larson; the great Michael Berry for giving me my first talk show; Mark Passwaters, Gerald Sanchez, and Brian McDonald for being great and loyal friends; Kenneth Fletcher for being the "Mighty Listener"; and to God, Whom I owe for everything.

And for any left off this list, I'll make sure to remember you for the sequel: *Bias in the Booth 2: Even More Biased!*

NOTES

CHAPTER ONE: LANDING ON TRAYVON

1. Michael Wallace, "The Heat Stand Tall for Trayvon Martin," *Miami Heat Index* (blog), ESPN.com, March 23, 2012, http://espn.go.com/blog/truehoop/miamiheat/post/_/id/13046/the-heat-stand-tall-for-trayvon-martin.

2. D. Kevin McNeir, "Crime Rate Drops but Murder Rate Now Five-Times the U.S. Average," *Miami Times*, October 31, 2013, http://miamitimesonline.com/news/2013/oct/31/crime-rate-drops-murder-rate-now-five-times-us-ave/.

3. Alexia Cooper and Erica L. Smith, *Homicide Trends in the United States, 1980–2008*, Bureau of Justice Statistics, U.S. Department of Justice, November 2011, pp. 3, 13. Available online at http://www.bjs.gov/content/pub/pdf/htus8008.pdf.

4.   Dave Hyde, "Heat's Photo a Powerful Statement," *Sun Sentinel*, March 24, 2012, http://articles.sun-sentinel.com/2012-03-24/sports/fl-hyde-miami-heat-hoodies-0325-20120324_1_wade-and-james-lebron-james-tweeted-voices.

5.   Benjamin Hochman, "LeBron's Message to the Masses Refreshing," *Denver Post*, March 25, 2012, http://www.denverpost.com/hochman/ci_20250341/lebrons-message-masses-refreshing.

6.   Jason Whitlock, "LeBron, Wade Show a Courageous Side," FoxSports.com, updated July 24, 2014, http://msn.foxsports.com/nba/story/LeBron-James-Dwyane-Wade-Miami-Heat-honor-Trayvon-Martin-shot-to-death-032412.

7.   Etan Thomas, "Athletes Take a Stand for President Obama," *The Root DC Live* (blog), *Washington Post*, August 28, 2012, http://www.washingtonpost.com/blogs/therootdc/post/president-obama-feels-the-love-from-a-new-generation-of-black-athletes/2012/08/28/4a392436-f143-11e1-a612-3cfc842a6d89_blog.html.

8.   "Jesse Jackson: Dan Gilbert Sees LeBron James as 'Runaway Slave,'" Huffington Post, July 11, 2010, updated May 25, 2011, http://www.huffingtonpost.com/2010/07/11/jesse-jackson-dan-gilbert_n_642363.html; and "Did Dan Gilbert Treat LeBron James like a 'Slave Master'? Is Mel Gibson Racist?," YouTube video, excerpt from July 12, 2010, episode of *The Joy Behar Show*, uploaded by Dr. Marc Lamont Hill, July 13, 2010, http://www.youtube.com/watch?v=yKbxYBPzrR0.

9.   Thomas, "Athletes Take a Stand for President Obama."

10. *State of the Union with Candy Crowley*, July 14, 2013, CNN.com, transcript, http://transcripts.cnn.com/TRANSCRIPTS/1307/14/sotu.02.html.

11. Susan Jones, "Liberal Law Prof: Zimmerman Case 'Should Never Have Been Brought in the First Place,'" CNSNews.com, July 15,

2013, http://cnsnews.com/news/article/liberal-law-prof-zimmerman-case-should-never-have-been-brought-first-place.

12. Dave Zirin, "'America's Justice System Is a Joke': Athletes Respond to Trayvon Martin Verdict," *Nation*, July 14, 2013, http://www.thenation.com/blog/175264/america-justice-system-joke-athletes-respond-trayvon-martin-verdict#.

13. Ibid.

14. Ibid.

15. Benjamin Chance, "Flashback: ESPN Abandoned Social Media Policy for Trayvon Martin Case," Breitbart Sports, Breitbart.com, July 16, 2013, http://www.breitbart.com/Breitbart-Sports/2013/07/16/FLASHBACK-ESPN-Abandoned-Social-Media-Policy-for-Trayvon-Martin-Case.

16. Ibid.

17. Ibid.

18. Lisa Suhay, "Should NFL Punish St. Louis Rams for 'Hands Up, Don't Shoot' Protest?," *Christian Science Monitor*, Yahoo! News UK and Ireland, December 1, 2014, https://uk.news.yahoo.com/nfl-punish-st-louis-rams-hands-dont-shoot-185555974.html#i3Zg9VM.

19. "Fisher: Rams Players Exercised Free Speech, Won't Be Disciplined," FoxSports.com, December 11, 2014, http://www.foxsports.com/nfl/story/st-louis-rams-ferguson-jeff-fisher-tavon-austin-brian-quick-jared-cook-stedman-bailey-120114.

20. Kevin Demoff, the executive vice president of the St. Louis Rams, announced this on Twitter. See the November 30, 2014, tweet here: https://twitter.com/kdemoff/status/539219554769960960.

21. "Sir Charles Barkley: The Last American Who Can Speak His Mind on Obama and Ferguson without Blowback," transcript

from the December 1, 2014, episode of *The Rush Limbaugh Show*, http://www.rushlimbaugh.com/daily/2014/12/01/sir_charles_ barkley_the_last_american_who_can_speak_his_mind_on_ obama_and_ferguson_without_blowback.

22. Tom Pelissero, "Dolphins' Don Jones Fined for Tweets about Michael Sam," *USA Today*, May 12, 2014, http://www.usatoday.com/story/ sports/nfl/dolphins/2014/05/11/don-jones-fined-for-michael-sam-tweets/8985297/.

23. Martin Rogers, "Niners CB Says Openly Gay Players Would Not Be Welcomed on the Team," Yahoo! Sports, January 30, 2013, http://sports.yahoo.com/news/nfl--report--niners-cb-says-openly-gay-players-would-not-be-welcomed-on-the-team-190346715.html.

24. Cam Inman "Culliver Says He Nor His Teammates Want Gay Teammate," *49ers Hot Read* (blog), MercuryNews.com, January 30, 2013, http://blogs.mercurynews.com/49ers/2013/01/30/report-culliver-says-gay-teammates-would-not-be-welcome/.

25. "Adam Silver Comments on 'I Can't Breathe' Pre-Game Warm-up Trend," TheSource.com, December 8, 2014, http://thesource.com/2014/12/08/adam-silver-comments-on-i-cant-breathe-pre-game-warm-up-trend/.

26. Mike Wells, "O'Neal's Elbow Wrap Costs 5k," IndyStar.com, November 12, 2006, http://www.indystar.com/apps/pbcs.dll/article?AID=/20061112/SPORTS04/611120445/1062/NLETTER01.

CHAPTER TWO:
THE SEPARATION OF CHURCH AND SPORT

1. Owen Ullmann, "Voices: Arizona's Anti-Gay Bill Is Shameful," *USA Today*, February 24, 2014, http://www.usatoday.com/story/news/nation/2014/02/24/voices-column-on-arizona-anti-gay-bill/5775081/.

2. "Arizona Anti-Gay Bill: Second Look," letters to the editor, *USA Today*, February 27, 2014, http://www.usatoday.com/story/opinion/2014/02/27/arizona-anti-gay-bill-second-look-your-say/5880025/.

3. "4 Things to Know about Arizona's 'Anti-Gay' Bill," *USA Today*, video, February 26, 2014, http://www.usatoday.com/videos/news/nation/2014/02/26/5830831/.

4. Mike Florio, "MLB Issues Strong Statement regarding Proposed Arizona Anti-Gay Law," ProFootballTalk.com, February 26, 2014, http://profootballtalk.nbcsports.com/2014/02/26/mlb-issues-strong-statement-regarding-arizona-anti-gay-law/.

5. Florio, "Arizona Governor Vetoes Anti-Gay Law, Clearing Path for Super Bowl XLIX," ProFootballTalk.com, February 26, 2014, http://profootballtalk.nbcsports.com/2014/02/26/arizona-governor-vetoes-anti-gay-law/.

6. David Steele, "Super Bowl Could Nix Arizona If It Doesn't Back Off Anti-Gay Law," *Sporting News*, updated February 25, 2014, http://www.sportingnews.com/nfl/story/2014-02-25/super-bowl-arizona-anti-gay-law-discrimination-deny-service-nfl-change-site-game-location.

7. Napp Nazworth, "Issue Analysis: Arizona Bill Does Not Give Businesses License to Discriminate against Gays," *Christian Post*, February 24, 2014, http://www.christianpost.com/news/issue-analysis-arizona-bill-does-not-give-businesses-license-to-discriminate-against-gays-115093/.

8. Paul Mirengoff, "No, This Is Not Jim Crow for Gays—Understanding Arizona SB 1062," *Powerline* (blog), February 25, 2014, http://www.powerlineblog.com/archives/2014/02/no-this-is-not-jim-crow-for-gays-understanding-arizona-s-b-1062.php.

9. Ibid.

10.   Daniel J. Flynn, "ESPN Overboard: Kornheiser Likens AZ Bill to Nazism," Breitbart Sports, Breitbart.com, February 27, 2014, http://www.breitbart.com/Breitbart-Sports/2014/02/27/Kornheiser-Likens-AZ-Bill-to-Nazism.

11.   Ibid.

12.   Ibid.

13.   Noel Sheppard, "Sports Radio Host Calls Tim Tebow's 'Lily White' NFL Draft Party a 'Nazi Rally,'" NewsBusters.org, April 24, 2010, http://newsbusters.org/blogs/noel-sheppard/2010/04/24/sports-radio-host-calls-tim-tebows-lily-white-nfl-draft-party-nazi-ra.

14.   Florio, "Russell Wilson Says He Was a 'Kind of a Bad Kid' Until He Found Religion," ProFootballTalk.com, October 17, 2013, http://profootballtalk.nbcsports.com/2013/10/17/russell-wilson-says-he-was-a-kind-of-a-bad-kid-until-he-found-religion/.

15.   Daniel Blake, "Gabby Douglas Praises God; Christian Gymnast Thankful After Winning All-Around Gold at Olympics 2012," *Christian Post*, August 2, 2012, http://www.christianpost.com/news/gabby-douglas-praises-god-christian-gymnast-thankful-after-winning-all-around-gold-at-olympics-2012-79386/.

16.   Ibid.

17.   Ibid.

18.   Matthew Dicker, "U.S. Women's Gymnastics Olympic Team 2012: Showcasing Effect Fab 5 Has on U.S.," BleacherReport.com, August 4, 2012, http://bleacherreport.com/articles/1284431-us-womens-gymnastics-olympic-team-2012-showcasing-effect-fab-5-has-on-us.

19.   Matt Yoder, "ESPN Dives Headfirst into the War on Christmas," AwfulAnnouncing.com, December 13, 2013, http://awfulannouncing.com/2013/espn-dives-headfirst-into-the-war-on-christmas.html.

20. The American Family Association sent out an "action alert" regarding the Craig James story, part of which is still available online at "Fox Sports Fires Sportscaster for His Christian Faith," FamilyandRelations. com, September 26, 2013, http://www.familyandrelations.com/ family-and-affairs/fox-sports-fires-sportscaster-for-his-christian-faith. html.

21. Barry Horn, "Craig James' Anti-Gay Stance during Political Campaign Reason for His Quick Exit from Fox Sports SW," SportsDayDFW, September 6, 2013, http://collegesportsblog. dallasnews.com/2013/09/craig-james-anti-gay-stance-during- political-campaign-reason-for-his-quick-exit-from-fssw-college- football-duties.html/.

22. Ben Shapiro, "Exclusive: Broadcaster Fired for Opposing Same-Sex Marriage Blasts Fox Sports for Religious Discrimination," Breitbart Sports, Breitbart.com, September 23, 2013, http://www. breitbart.com/Breitbart-Sports/2013/09/23/Craig-Jones-Fox- Sports-gay-marriage.

23. Ibid.

24. Horn, "Craig James' Anti-Gay Stance."

25. Shapiro, "Exclusive: Broadcaster Fired for Opposing Same-Sex Marriage."

26. Richard Langford, "Jason Whitlock Shows True Colors on Twitter with Lame Jeremy Lin Tweet," BleacherReport.com, February 14, 2014, http://bleacherreport.com/articles/1066390-jason-whitlock- shows-true-colors-on-twitter-with-lame-jeremy-lin-tweet.

27. Scott Whitlock, "The Worst of the Worst: A Look Back at Keith Olbermann's Most Outrageous Quotes," NewsBusters.org, January 24, 2011, http://newsbusters.org/blogs/scott-whitlock/2011/01/24/ worst-worst-look-back-keith-olbermanns-most-outrageous-quotes.

28. Ibid.

29. Ibid.

30. ESPN.com News Services, "Ron Brown: 'Views Stand the Same,'" ESPN.com, May 8, 2012, http://espn.go.com/college-football/story/_/id/7896560/nebraska-cornhuskers-assistant-coach-ron-brown-says-job-safe-curb-anti-gay-stance.

31. Gene Wojciechowski, "Ron Brown Confusing Faith with Rights," ESPN.com, April 27, 2012, http://espn.go.com/college-football/story/_/id/7863307/nebraska-cornhuskers-assistant-ron-brown-confusing-faith-rights.

32. Paul Wilson, "Why Are Christian Athletes Still Being Crucified by Sports Media?," FoxNews.com, September 5, 2012, http://www.foxnews.com/opinion/2012/09/05/why-are-christian-athletes-still-being-crucified-by-sports-media/.

33. Anthony Witrado, "Torii Hunter Would Be 'Uncomfortable' with Having a Gay Teammate," *Sporting News*, updated December 30, 2012, http://www.sportingnews.com/mlb/story/2012-12-30/torii-hunter-comments-gay-teammate-detroit-tigers-mlb-locker-room.

34. Dayn Perry, "Torii Hunter: Having Gay Teammate Would Be 'Difficult,'" CBSSports.com, December 30, 2012, http://www.cbssports.com/mlb/eye-on-baseball/21474369/torii-hunter-having-gay-teammate-would-be-.

35. Matthew Philbin, "'Glee' on the Gridiron?," NewsBusters.com, March 20, 2013, http://newsbusters.org/blogs/matthew-philbin/2013/03/20/glee-gridiron.

36. Gayle Falkenthal, "Manny Pacquiao Takes a Punch over Gay Marriage Remarks," Communities, *Washington Times*, May 16, 2012, http://communities.washingtontimes.com/neighborhood/ringside-seat/2012/may/16/manny-pacquiao-takes-punch-over-gay-marriage-remar/.

37. "Manny Pacquiao against Same-Sex Marriage but Never Said Gay People 'Must Be Put to Death,'" Huffington Post, May 16, 2012, http://www.huffingtonpost.com/2012/05/16/manny-pacquiao-gay-marriage-leviticus-examiner_n_1521747.html.

38. Twitchy staff, "Lefties Call for Nike to Drop Manny Pacquiaofor 'Homophobic' Remarks He *Never Made*; Update: Pacquiao Banned from LA Mall for Life," Twitchy.com, May 16, 2012, http://twitchy.com/2012/05/16/lefties-call-for-nike-to-drop-manny-pacquiao-for-homophobic-remarks-he-never-made/.

39. Ibid.

40. "Manny Pacquiao against Same-Sex Marriage but Never Said Gay People 'Must Be Put to Death,'" Huffington Post.

41. Falkenthal, "Manny Pacquiao Takes a Punch over Gay Marriage Remarks."

42. Twitchy staff, "Lefties Call for Nike to Drop Manny Pacquiao."

43. Ibid.

44. Laurel Fantauzzo, "An Open Letter to Manny Pacquiao from a Gay Filipina American," *Grantland* (blog), May 17, 2012, http://grantland.com/features/an-open-letter-manny-pacquiao-gay-filipina-american-concerning-champion-boxer-recent-comments-gay-marriage/.

45. Matthew Balan, "ESPN to Manny Pacquiao: Stop Defending 'Cruel, Untrue' Catholic Church," NewsBusters.com, May 19, 2012, http://newsbusters.org/blogs/matthew-balan/2012/05/19/espn-manny-pacquiao-stop-defending-cruel-untrue-catholic-church.

46. Daniel King, "'Keep God Out of Football'—Fifa Tells Brazil's Soccer Superstars," *Daily Mail*, July 12, 2009, http://www.dailymail.co.uk/news/article-1199121/Brazils-football-superstars-told-Keep-faith-football.html.

47. Ibid.

48. Ibid.

49. "Fifa Allows Wearing of Head Covers for Religious Reasons," BBC.com, March 1, 2014, http://www.bbc.com/sport/0/ football/26398297.

50. Ibid.

51. Jeré Longman, "For Lolo Jones, Everything Is Image," *New York Times*, August 4, 2012, http://www.nytimes.com/2012/08/05/ sports/olympics/olympian-lolo-jones-draws-attention-to-beauty- not-achievement.html?_r=0.

52. John Branch, "NFL Prospect Michael Sam Proudly Says What Teammates Knew: He's Gay," *New York Times*, February 10, 2014, http://www.nytimes.com/2014/02/10/sports/michael-sam- college-football-star-says-he-is-gay-ahead-of-nfl-draft.html.

53. "Michael Sam Meets with Dallas Cowboys," YouTube video, 2:51, excerpt from September 3, 2014, episode of ESPN's *First Take*, uploaded by "ESPN1stTake," September 3, 2014, https://www. youtube.com/watch?v=Z_Xx6aqRhmo#t=21.

54. Al Weaver, "Report: NFL Officials Asked Teams to Consider Signing Michael Sam to Practice Squad," Daily Caller, September 4, 2014, http://dailycaller.com/2014/09/04/report-nfl-officials- asked-teams-to-consider-signing-michael-sam-to-practice-squad/.

CHAPTER THREE: KNAVES ON THE WARPATH

1. Sarah Kogod, "Bob Costas on Redskins Name: 'It's an Insult, a Slur,'" *Washington Post*, October 13, 2013, http://www. washingtonpost.com/blogs/dc-sports-bog/wp/2013/10/13/bob- costas-on-redskins-name-its-an-insult-a-slur/.

2. Associated Press, "UND OK to Drop Fighting Sioux Name," ESPN.com, June 14, 2012, http://espn.go.com/college-sports/

story/_/id/8045554/north-dakota-residents-vote-let-school-scrap-fighting-sioux-nickname.

3. Associated Press, "How Many Native Americans Think 'Redskins' Is a Slur?," Washington.CBSLocal.com, October 8, 2013, http://washington.cbslocal.com/2013/10/08/how-many-native-americans-think-redskins-is-a-slur/.

4. "Letter from Washington Redskins Owner Dan Snyder to Fans," *Washington Post*, October 9, 2013, http://www.washingtonpost.com/local/letter-from-washington-redskins-owner-dan-snyder-to-fans/2013/10/09/e7670ba0-30fe-11e3-8627-c5d7de0a046b_story.html.

5. "Dan Patrick: Owner Snyder Will Change Redskins Name," Breitbart Sports, Breitbart.com, October 14, 2013, http://www.breitbart.com/Breitbart-Sports/2013/10/14/Dan-Patrick-Snyder-Will-Change-Name.

6. Erik Brady, "Daniel Snyder Says Redskins Will Never Change Name," *USA Today*, May 10, 2013, http://www.usatoday.com/story/sports/nfl/redskins/2013/05/09/washington-redskins-daniel-snyder/2148127/.

7. "The Fighting Whities—American Morning with Paula Zahn, March 13, 2002," YouTube video, excerpt from March 13, 2002, episode of CNN's *American Morning*, uploaded by "Countdown Fan," December 22, 2011, http://www.youtube.com/watch?v=B_mzZRX-JVQ.

8. Ibid.

9. Clarence Page, "Fightin' Whities Mascot Raises a Little Awareness, a Little Cash," SeattlePi, March 18, 2002, http://www.seattlepi.com/news/article/Fightin-Whities-mascot-raises-a-little-awarness-1083127.php.

10.   Dylan Gwinn, "Why Chief Wahoo's Caucasian Brother Doesn't Bother White People," Breitbart Sports, Breitbart.com, August 18, 2014, http://www.breitbart.com/Breitbart-Sports/2014/08/18/Hail-to-the-Chief.

11.   Peter Edward, "'Caucasians' T-Shirt Mocking Cleveland Indians Becomes Hot Seller on Reserves," *Toronto Star*, July 29, 2014, http://www.thestar.com/sports/2014/07/29/caucasians_tshirt_mocking_cleveland_indians_becomes_hot_seller_on_reserves.html.

12.   Craig Calcaterra, "'Caucasians' T-Shirts Are Hot Sellers on Canadian Indian Reservations," *Hardball Talk* (blog), NBCSports.com, July 29, 2014, http://hardballtalk.nbcsports.com/2014/07/29/caucasians-t-shirts-are-hot-sellers-on-canadian-indian-reservations/.

13.   Felicia Fonseca, "Judge Dismisses Charges against Navajo President," *News from Indian Country*, February 2011, http://www.indiancountrynews.com/news/9-news-from-through-out-indian-country/11042-judge-dismisses-charges-against-navajo-president.

14.   Barry Petchesky, "Disgraced, Soon-to-Be-Former-Navajo Nation President Attends 'Skins Game," *Deadspin* (blog), October 12, 2014, http://deadspin.com/disgraced-soon-to-be-former-navajo-nation-president-at-1645509844.

15.   Daniel J. Flynn, "Navajo Nation President Watches Redskins Game with Dan Snyder," Breitbart Sports, Breitbart.com, October 13, 2014, http://www.breitbart.com/Breitbart-Sports/2014/10/13/Navajo-Nation-President-in-Redskins-Box.

16.   Dave McKenna, "No Name Is Really Sacred to Dan Snyder," *Deadspin* (blog), June 25, 2014, http://deadspin.com/no-name-is-really-sacred-to-dan-snyder-1595841512.

17.   Sean Newell, "President Obama: I'd 'Think about Changing' Redskins Nickname," *Deadspin* (blog), October 6, 2013, http://

deadspin.com/president-obama-id-think-about-changing-redskins-ni-1441711555.

18.   "Oneida: Central New York," Christian Peacemaker Teams, no date, http://www.cpt.org/work/aboriginal_justice/Oneida.

19.   Daniel Greenfield, "Casino Kingpin and Fake Indian Chief Targets Redskins," FrontPageMag.com, October 8, 2013, http://www.frontpagemag.com/2013/dgreenfield/casino-kingpin-and-fake-indian-chief-targets-redskins/.

20.   "Oneida: Central New York," Christian Peacemaker Teams.

21.   *Shenandoah et al. v. Halbritter,* synopsis and description available at http://ccrjustice.org/ourcases/past-cases/shenandoah,-et-al.-v.-halbritter.

22.   "The Oneidas For Democracy: Who We Are," Oneidas for Democracy, no date, http://www.oneidasfordemocracy.org/main/the-oneidas-for-democracy-who-we-are/.

CHAPTER FOUR: MAKING A HERO OF MICHAEL SAM

1.   Stewart Mandel, "Michael Sam Breaks Longstanding Barrier by Announcing He Is Gay," *Sports Illustrated,* updated June 11, 2014, http://www.si.com/nfl/2014/02/10/michael-sam-missouri-tigers-nfl-draft.

2.   Glenn McGraw, "Michael Sam Comes Out as Gay: Fans and Media React on Twitter," GameDayR.com, February 9, 2014, http://gamedayr.com/sports/michael-sam-gay-twitter-reactions-97478/.

3.   Ibid.

4.   Ibid.

5.   Ibid.

6.   Pete Prisco, "Tebow Throws Out Some, but Not All Doubts," Real Clear Sports, March 18, 2010, http://www.realclearsports.

com/2010/03/18/tebow_throws_out_some_but_not_all_
doubts_71824.html.

7.   Jerry Spar, "Pete Prisco on D&C: Tim Tebow 'Stinks,' Will Be Cut
by Patriots in Mid-August," *It Is What It Is* (blog), June 11, 2013,
http://itiswhatitis.weei.com/sports/newengland/football/
patriots/2013/06/11/pete-prisco-on-dc-tim-tebow-stinks-will-be-
cut-by-patriots-in-mid-august/.

8.   Jeff Pearlman, "I Want Tim Tebow to Fail," *Jeff Pearlman* (blog),
February 2, 2010, http://www.jeffpearlman.com/i-want-tim-tebow-to-fail/.

9.   Ibid.

10. Pearlman, "Dmitriy Salita," *Jeff Pearlman* (blog), October 18,
2012, http://www.jeffpearlman.com/the-quaz-qa-dmitriy-salita/.

11. Ibid.

12. Pearlman, "Michael Sam," *Jeff Pearlman* (blog), February 10,
2014, http://www.jeffpearlman.com/michael-sam/.

13. Dave Zirin, "Why the Curious Right-Wing Silence on Michael
Sam?," *Nation*, February 13, 2014, http://www.thenation.com/
blog/178377/why-curious-right-wing-silence-michael-sam.

14. "Sports Anchor Blasts Michael Sam Critics, Calls Out Conservative
Hypocrisy," Mediaite, February 12, 2014, http://www.mediaite.
com/tv/sports-anchor-blasts-michael-sam-critics-calls-out-
conservative-hypocrisy/.

15. "How Will News That Michael Sam Is Gay Affect His NFL Draft
Stock?," *Sports Illustrated*, February 9, 2014, http://www.si.com/
football/2014/02/09/michael-sam-draft-stock.

16. "Texas Anchor Amy Kushnir Throws Hilarious On-Air Temper
Tantrum over Michael Sam Kiss," Queerty, May 14, 2014, http://
www.queerty.com/texas-anchor-amy-kushnir-throws-hilarious-
on-air-temper-tantrum-over-michael-sam-kiss-20140514; Sean
Pendergast, "Zapruder Analysis of Four Dallas TV Women
Verbally Brawling over Michael Sam," HoustonPress.com, May

15, 2014, http://blogs.houstonpress.com/news/2014/05/zapruder_
analysis_of_four_dall.php; and Cindy Boren, "Watch Dallas TV
Host Walk off Set during Debate on Michael Sam Kiss,"
Washington Post, May 15, 2014, http://www.washingtonpost.
com/blogs/early-lead/wp/2014/05/15/watch-dallas-tv-host-walk-
off-set-during-debate-on-michael-sam-kiss/.

17. Ibid.
18. John Breech, "Dolphins Fine and Suspend DB Don Jones for
Anti-Michael Sam Tweet," CBSSports.com, May 11, 2014, http://
www.cbssports.com/nfl/eye-on-football/24559187/dolphins-db-
don-jones-fined-suspended-for-anti-michael-sam-tweet.
19. Mike Wise, "Jason Collins's Religious Critics Need to Practice
What They Preach," *Washington Post*, April 30, 2013, http://
www.washingtonpost.com/sports/wizards/jason-collins-religious-
critics-need-to-practice-what-they-preach/2013/04/30/3129e752-
b1df-11e2-9a98-4be1688d7d84_story.html.
20. Ibid.
21. Ibid.
22. Phil Mushnick, "Being a Great Player Doesn't Make Peterson a
Great Guy," *New York Post*, October 13, 2013, http://nypost.
com/2013/10/13/sons-death-doesnt-make-adrian-peterson-a-great-
person/?utm_source=SFnewyorkpost&utm_medium=SF
newyorkpost.
23. Barry Petchesky, "Your Regular Reminder That Phil Mushnick Is
a Race-Baiting Troll," *Deadspin* (blog), October 14, 2013, http://
deadspin.com/your-regular-reminder-that-phil-mushnick-is-a-race-
bait-1445099979.
24. Reva Friedel, "Phil Mushnick Wrote the Most Offensive Sports
Column in the History of the Earth," AwfulAnnouncing.com,
October 14, 2013, http://awfulannouncing.com/2013/phil-mushnick-
wrote-the-most-offensive-sports-column-in-the-history-of-earth.html.

25. Wise, "Jason Collins's Religious Critics."

26. Matthew Philbin, "Into Left Field: 5 of the Most Obnoxious Political Intrusions on Sports," NewsBusters.org, April 3, 2014, http://newsbusters.org/blogs/matthew-philbin/2014/04/03/left-field-5-most-obnoxious-political-intrusions-sports.

27. "Gregg Doyel," Muckrack.com, http://muckrack.com/gregg-doyel/statuses/436533856800636928.

28. Gregg Doyel, "Constant Media Attention Could Derail Sam's Career Just Like Tebow's," CBSSports.com, February 20, 2014, http://www.cbssports.com/general/writer/gregg-doyel/24449523/constant-media-attention-could-derail-sams-career-just-like-tebows.

29. Philbin, "Into Left Field."

30. Austin Ruse, "Gay Speech Police Targets Giants for Hiring Super Bowl Hero," Breitbart Sports, Breitbart.com, July 23, 2014, http://www.breitbart.com/Breitbart-Sports/2014/07/23/Super-Bowl-Hero-Targeted.

31. Ibid.

32. Ibid.

33. Michael O'Keeffe, "David Tyree, Who Said He'd Trade Super Bowl If It Meant Stopping Gay Marriage, Joins NY Giants as Director of Player Development," *New York Daily News*, updated July 22, 2014, http://www.nydailynews.com/sports/football/giants/david-tyree-returns-ny-giants-director-player-development-article-1.1876104; and A. J. Perez, "David Tyree, Giants New Staffer, Says He Knows 'Former Homosexuals,'" NJ.com, updated July 24, 2014, http://www.nj.com/giants/index.ssf/2014/07/david_tyree_giants_new_staffer_says_he_knows_former_homosexuals.html.

34. Charlie Joughin, "When Did David Tyree Decide to Be Straight?," *HRC Blog*, Human Rights Campaign, July 22, 2014, http://www. hrc.org/blog/entry/when-did-david-tyree-decide-to-be-straight.

35. O'Keeffe, "David Tyree, Who Said He'd Trade Super Bowl If It Meant Stopping Gay Marriage, Joins NY Giants as Director of Player Development."

36. Wade Davis, "Only Love Drives Out Hate," Monday Morning Quarterback, Sports Illustrated, July 24, 2014, http://mmqb.si. com/2014/07/24/new-york-giants-david-tyree-gay-comments-wade-davis/.

37. Bernie Augustine, "Chris Kluwe Says He Was Cut by Vikings over Stance on Gay Marriage, Calls Special Teams Coach a Bigot," *New York Daily News*, updated January 3, 2014, http://www. nydailynews.com/sports/football/kluwe-vikes-cut-gay-marriage-advocacy-article-1.1564805.

38. Chris Kluwe, "I Was an NFL Player Until I Was Fired by Two Cowards and a Bigot," *Deadspin* (blog), January 2, 2014, http://deadspin.com/i-was-an-nfl-player-until-i-was-fired-by-two-cowards-an-1493208214.

39. Vikings PR, "Vikings Respond to Independent Investigative Report of Chris Kluwe's Allegations," Vikings.com, July 18, 2014, http://www.vikings.com/news/article-1/Vikings-Respond-To-Independent-Investigative-Report-of-Chris-Kluwes-Allegations/207d9d67-eda5-45e7-bed2-8adcd8df113a.

40. Ibid.

41. Ibid.

42. Mike Florio, "Vikings Begin to Push Back against Kluwe," ProFootballTalk.com, July 18, 2014, http://profootballtalk. nbcsports.com/2014/07/18/vikings-begin-to-push-back-against-kluwe/.

43. Bobby Bonett, "Chris Kluwe Addresses 'Compromising Situation' Tweet on NFL Radio," *Sirius XM Blog: Sports*, July 22, 2014, http://blog.siriusxm.com/2014/07/22/chris-kluwe-addresses-compromising-situation-tweet/.

44. Doyel, "Chris Kluwe Can't Be a Moral Crusader after His Cruel Twitter Rant," CBSSports.com, July 19, 2014, http://www.cbssports.com/general/writer/gregg-doyel/24628550/chris-kluwe-cant-be-moral-crusader-after-his-cruel-twitter-rant.

45. Robert Wilde, "Chris Kluwe Drops Suit; Vikings Donate to LGBT Groups," Breitbart Sports, Breitbart.com, August 20, 2014, http://www.breitbart.com/Breitbart-Sports/2014/08/19/Chris-Kluwe-Drops-Lawsuit-With-Vikings-over-Homophobic-Claims.

CHAPTER FIVE: TRASHING TEBOW

1. Gregg Rosenthal, "Tebow's Pre-Wonderlic Prayer Request Falls Flat," ProFootballTalk.com, March 23, 2010, http://profootballtalk.nbcsports.com/2010/03/23/tebows-pre-wonderlic-prayer-request-falls-flat/.

2. Ibid.

3. Ibid.

4. Rosenthal, "Tebow Denies Wonderlic Incident," ProFootballTalk.com, March 24, 2010, http://profootballtalk.nbcsports.com/2010/03/24/tebow-denies-wonderlic-incident/.

5. "Sresnick," "Broker: Manziel Got $7,500 for Autographs," ESPN1005.com, updated August 6, 2013, http://espn1005.com/archives/37586.

6. Simone Wilson, "Video: Kobe Bryant Throws Towel, Mouths 'Faggot' to Ref at Lakers-Spurs Game," LAWeekly.com, April 13, 2011, http://www.laweekly.com/informer/2011/04/13/video-kobe-bryant-throws-towel-mouths-faggot-to-ref-at-lakers-spurs-game.

7. Woody Paige, "Paige: Broncos' Tim Tebow Dealing with Tension, Frustration," *Denver Post*, August 5, 2011, http://www.denverpost.com/ci_18621060?source=infinite.

8. Gregg Doyel, "Unbelievable—Tebow Believes Faith Equates to Starting in the NFL," CBSSports.com, August 6, 2011, http://www.cbssports.com/columns/story/15406131/unbelievable-tebow-believes-faith-equates-to-starting-in-nfl.

9. Ibid.

10. Ibid.

11. Ibid.

12. Ibid.

13. "2009 Kurt Warner and Jesus," YouTube video, uploaded by "wwensek," January 19, 2009, http://www.youtube.com/watch?v=MdTLqmY5x3M&feature=related.

14. Dan Bickley, "Kurt Warner to Tim Tebow: Let Your Actions Be Your Words," AZCentral.com, November 26, 2011, http://www.azcentral.com/sports/cardinals/articles/2011/11/26/20111126nfl-kurt-warner-tim-tebow-advice.html.

15. Todd Starnes, "Why Are Anti-Christian Bigots So Eager to Prey on Tim Tebow?," FoxNews.com, December 12, 2011, http://www.foxnews.com/opinion/2011/12/12/why-are-anti-christian-bigots-so-eager-to-prey-on-tim-tebow/.

16. Brian Ives, "Interview: Gene Simmons Defends Tim Tebow, Wants Football to Be More like KISS," Radio.com, September 13, 2013, http://radio.com/2013/09/13/gene-simmons-tim-tebow-religion-football-interview/.

17. Mark Cannizzaro, "Smith, Dungy, Edwards at Head of Classy Table," *New York Post*, January 23, 2007, http://nypost.com/2007/01/23/smith-dungy-edwards-at-head-of-classy-table/.

18. John Branch, "Two Coaches, Two Friends, but Only One Prize," *New York Times*, February 5, 2007, http://www.nytimes.com/2007/02/05/sports/football/05branch.html?ref=tonydungy&_r=1&.

19. Ibid.

20. Associated Press, "CBS Urged to Scrap Tebow Ad," ESPN.com, updated January 25, 2012, http://sports.espn.go.com/nfl/playoffs/2009/news/story?id=4857753.

21. Paul Wilson, "NFL Analysts: Tim Tebow Hated Because of His Faith," NewsBusters.org, October 21, 2011, http://newsbusters.org/blogs/paul-wilson/2011/10/21/nfl-analysts-tim-tebow-hated-because-his-faith.

22. "Tell Us: Is Tebow Victim of Anti-Religious Bias?," GameOn!, *USA Today*, August 24, 2011, http://content.usatoday.com/communities/gameon/post/2011/08/tell-us-is-tebow-backlash-religious-based/1#uslPageReturn.

23. Wilson, "NFL Analysts: Tim Tebow Hated Because of His Faith."

CHAPTER SIX: CONCUSSED AND CONFUSED

1. See Dan Wolken's January 13, 2014, tweet here: https://twitter.com/DanWolken/status/422726109726142465.

2. See Wolken's January 13, 2014, tweet here: https://twitter.com/DanWolken/status/422730082893836288.

3. "2013 Rating Wrap: NFL Dominates List of Most Watched Sporting Events," December 2013, SportsMediaWatch.com, http://www.sportsmediawatch.com/2013/12/2013-ratings-wrap-nfl-dominates-list-of-most-watched-sporting-events/.

4. Richard Sandomir, "ESPN Extends Deal with N.F.L. for $15 Billion," *New York Times*, September 8, 2011, http://www.nytimes.com/2011/09/09/sports/football/espn-extends-deal-with-nfl-for-15-billion.html.

5.   James Andrew Miller and Ken Belson, "N.F.L. Pressure Said to Lead ESPN to Quit Film Project," *New York Times*, August 23, 2013, http://www.nytimes.com/2013/08/24/sports/football/nfl-pressure-said-to-prompt-espn-to-quit-film-project.html?smid=tw-share&_r=1.

6.   "Gladwell: Why College Football Is like Dog Fighting," excerpt from Malcolm Gladwell interview on *Global Public Square*, CNN.com, July 20, 2013, http://globalpublicsquare.blogs.cnn.com/2013/07/20/gladwell-why-college-football-is-like-dog-fighting/.

7.   David DiSalvo, "Is Malcolm Gladwell Right, Should College Football Be Banned to Save Brains?," *Forbes*, July 21, 2013, http://www.forbes.com/sites/daviddisalvo/2013/07/21/is-malcolm-gladwell-right-should-college-football-be-banned/.

8.   Daniel J. Flynn, "The NFL Suicide Epidemic Myth," Breitbart Sports, Breitbart.com, January 13, 2014, http://www.breitbart.com/Breitbart-Sports/2014/01/12/The-NFL-Suicide-Epidemic-Myth.

9.   Ibid.

10. Ibid.

11. Ibid.

12. Sally Jenkins, "No Matter What Happens in NFL Labor Negotiations, the Players Pay the Price," *Washington Post*, February 23, 2011, http://www.washingtonpost.com/wp-dyn/content/article/2011/02/23/AR2011022305999.html.

13. Frank Bruni, "Pro Football's Violent Toll," *New York Times*, December 4, 2012, http://www.nytimes.com/2012/12/04/opinion/bruni-pro-footballs-violent-toll.html?_r=0.

14. Don Banks, "What Price Football?," Monday Morning Quarterback, *Sports Illustrated*, October 23, 2013, http://mmqb.si.com/2013/10/23/price-of-concussions-don-banks/.

15. Bob Ryan, "Football a Game of Inherent Conflict," *Boston Globe*, November 17, 2013, http://www.bostonglobe.com/sports/2013/11/17/football-game-inherent-conflict/GkAXWtEoJWdjEoqH0dHIAJ/story.html.

16. Ibid.

17. Ibid.

18. Ibid.

19. Steve Fainaru and Mark Fainaru-Wada, "Youth Football Participation Drops," ESPN.com, updated November 4, 2013, http://espn.go.com/espn/otl/story/_/page/popwarner/pop-warner-youth-football-participation-drops-nfl-concussion-crisis-seen-causal-factor.

20. Jarrett Bell, "Study Shows NFL Players Live Longer," *USA Today*, updated May 9, 2012, http://usatoday30.usatoday.com/sports/football/nfl/story/2012-05-08/Study-shows-NFL-players-live-longer/54847564/1.

21. Ibid.

22. "Do Sports Concussions Really Cause Chronic Traumatic Encephalopathy?," Newswire, Loyola Medicine, December 2, 2013, http://www.loyolamedicine.org/newswire/news/do-sports-concussions-really-cause-chronic-traumatic-encephalopathy.

23. Ibid.

CHAPTER SEVEN: BLACKLISTING LIMBAUGH

1. ESPN.com News Services, "Limbaugh's Comments Touch Off Controversy," ESPN.com, October 1, 2013, http://sports.espn.go.com/nfl/news/story?id=1627887.

2. "NFL Player Passing Statistics—2003," ESPN.com, http://espn.go.com/nfl/statistics/player/_/stat/passing/sort/passingYards/year/2003.

3.   ESPN.com News Services, "McNabb: Too Late for an Apology from Limbaugh," ESPN.com, updated October 1, 2003, http://sports.espn.go.com/espn/wire?id=1627977.

4.   Ibid.

5.   Ibid.

6.   ESPN.com News Services, "Limbaugh Resigns from NFL Show," ESPN.com, October 2, 2003, http://espn.go.com/gen/news/2003/1001/1628537.html.

7.   ESPN.com News Services, "McNabb: Too Late for an Apology from Limbaugh," ESPN.com, updated October 1, 2003, http://sports.espn.go.com/espn/wire?id=1627977.

8.   ESPN.com News Services, "Limbaugh Resigns from ESPN's NFL Pregame Show," ESPN.com, October 2, 2003, http://espn.go.com/gen/news/2003/1002/1628778.html.

9.   Ralph Vacchiano, "In No Rush to Forget: McNabb's Dad Still Irate over Limbaugh's Attack," *New York Daily News*, January 18, 2004, http://www.nydailynews.com/archives/sports/rush-forget-mcnabb-dad-irate-limbaugh-attack-article-1.605662.

10. Allen Barra, "Rush Limbaugh Was Right," Slate, October 2, 2003, http://www.slate.com/articles/sports/sports_nut/2003/10/rush_limbaugh_was_right.html.

11. Noel Sheppard, "Wilbon: Rush Limbaugh 'Universally Reviled by African-Americans,'" NewsBusters.org, October 18, 2009, http://newsbusters.org/blogs/noel-sheppard/2009/10/18/wilbon-rush-limbaugh-universally-reviled-african-americans.

12. Sheppard, "Sportswriter: Black NFLers Claiming They Won't Play for Rush 'Are Lying through Their Teeth,'" NewsBusters.org, October 12, 2009, http://newsbusters.org/blogs/noel-sheppard/2009/10/12/sportswriter-black-nflers-claiming-they-wont-play-rush-are-lying-thro.

13. Ibid.

14. "ESPN Bigots Obsessed with Rush," RushLimbaugh.com, transcript from January 24, 2007, episode of *The Rush Limbaugh Show*, http://www.rushlimbaugh.com/daily/2007/01/24/espn_bigots_obsessed_with_rush.

15. Sheppard, "Wilbon: Rush Limbaugh 'Universally Reviled by African-Americans.'"

16. "The National Hemorrhoid Pops Up, Claims Criticism of Obama Is Racist," transcript from the September 16, 2009, episode of *The Rush Limbaugh Show*, http://img.rushlimbaugh.com/home/daily/site_091609/content/01125106.guest.html.

17. Tim Graham, "Ed Schultz Decries 'Age of Overzealous Law Enforcement,' Guest Calls Gates 'Rosa Parks' of Profiling," NewsBusters.org, July 24, 2009, http://newsbusters.org/blogs/tim-graham/2009/07/24/ed-schultz-decries-age-overzealous-law-enforcement-guest-calls-gates-ros.

18. "Michael Eric Dyson," entry on DiscovertheNetworks.org, accessed September 2014, http://www.discoverthenetworks.org/individualProfile.asp?indid=2192.

19. Debbie Schlussel, "Not Sharp, Drew: *USA Today*/Freep Sportswriter Used Fake *Wikipedia* Quotes to Savage Limbaugh," DebbieSchlussel.com, October 13, 2009, http://www.debbieschlussel.com/10335/not-sharp-drew-usa-todayfreep-sportswriter-used-fake-wikipedia-quotes-to-savage-limbaugh/.

20. Ohm Youngmisuk, "Black NFL Players Crush Prospect of Playing for a Rush Limbaugh–Owned St. Louis Rams," *New York Daily News*, October 9, 2009, http://www.nydailynews.com/sports/football/black-nfl-players-crush-prospect-playing-rush-limbaugh-owned-st-louis-rams-article-1.383689.

21. Ibid.

22. Mike Fitzpatrick, "Bill Maher Buys Minority Share in New York Mets," Associated Press, Huffington Post Sports, updated August 3, 2012, http://www.huffingtonpost.com/2012/06/03/bill-maher-new-york-mets-owner-minority-share-video_n_1566669.html.

23. Adam Rubin, "Bill Maher Owns Stake in Mets," ESPN.com, June 4, 2012, http://espn.go.com/new-york/mlb/story/_/id/8004806/bill-maher-reveals-owns-minority-share-new-york-mets.

24. Associated Press, "Checketts, Limbaugh in Bid to Buy Rams," ESPN.com, updated October 6, 2009, http://sports.espn.go.com/nfl/news/story?id=4535583.

25. George Vecsey, "32 Voices Louder Than Limbaugh's," *New York Times*, October 13, 2009, http://www.nytimes.com/2009/10/13/sports/football/13vecsey.html?_r=0.

26. Zach Berman and Richard Sandomir, "Bill Maher Now Owns Share of the Mets," *New York Times*, June 4, 2012, http://www.nytimes.com/2012/06/04/sports/baseball/bill-maher-now-owns-share-of-the-mets.html.

27. Ibid.

28. "Bill Maher Compares Retarded Children to Dogs," YouTube video, excerpt from January 11, 2001, episode of *Politically Correct*, uploaded by "jvideos8," October 4, 2007, https://www.youtube.com/watch?v=Xe57F77ZKIs.

29. Ibid.

30. "Maher: Obama Not Acting like a Real Black President," Real Clear Politics, May 29, 2010, http://www.realclearpolitics.com/video/2010/05/29/maher_obama_not_acting_like_a_real_black_president.html.

CHAPTER EIGHT: BULL IN DURHAM

1. Scott Whitlock, "ABC Looks at Media Bias in Duke Rape Case; Ignores Example from Own Network," NewsBusters.org, September 4, 2007, http://newsbusters.org/blogs/scott-whitlock/2007/09/04/abc-looks-media-bias-duke-rape-case-ignores-example-own-network.

2. KC Johnson, "Feinstein: 'They're Probably Guilty of Everything but Rape,'" *Durham-in-Wonderland* (blog), May 7, 2007, http://durhamwonderland.blogspot.com/2007/05/feinstein-theyre-probably-guilty-of.html.

3. Johnson, "John Feinstein, and the Unbearable Lightness of America's Sportswriters," *Durham-in-Wonderland* (blog), June 5, 2007, http://durhamwonderland.blogspot.com/2007/06/john-feinstein-and-unbearable-lightness.html.

4. Selena Roberts, "Sports of the Times; When Peer Pressure, Not a Conscience, Is Your Guide," *New York Times*, March 31, 2006, http://query.nytimes.com/gst/fullpage.html?res=9D04E0DC1230F932A05750C0A9609C8B63; and Johnson, "Selena Roberts: Still Misleading," *Durham-in-Wonderland* (blog), March 17, 2008, http://durhamwonderland.blogspot.com/2008/03/selena-roberts-still-misleading.html.

5. John Leo, "A 'Wildly Misleading' Self-Defense," Minding the Campus, March 18, 2008, http://www.mindingthecampus.com/2008/03/a_wildly_misleading_selfdefens/.

6. Johnson, "Her 'Great Job Covering Rape Culture,'" Minding the Campus, March 10, 2014, http://www.mindingthecampus.com/2014/03/her_great_job_covering_rape_cu/.

7. Johnson, "Selena Roberts & Journalistic Credibility," *Durham-in-Wonderland* (blog), May 4, 2009, http://durhamwonderland.blogspot.com/2009/05/selena-roberts-journalistic-credibility.html.

8. Ibid.

9. Roberts, "Closing a Case Will Not Mean Closure at Duke," *New York Times*, March 25, 2007, http://www.nytimes.com/2007/03/25/sports/othersports/25roberts.html?_r=0.

10. xy109e3, "The Edwards-Marcotte Fiasco," *Daily Kos* (blog), February 2, 2007, http://www.dailykos.com/story/2007/02/02/297671/-The-Edwards-Marcotte-Fiasco.

11. Stuart Taylor Jr., "Witness for the Prosecution? The *New York Times* Is Still Victimizing Innocent Dukies," Slate, August 29, 2006, http://www.slate.com/articles/news_and_politics/hey_wait_a_minute/2006/08/witness_for_the_prosecution.single.html.

12. John Koblin, "Who's 'This Lady'? Meet Selena Roberts, A-Rod's Worst Nightmare," *New York Observer*, February 11, 2009, http://observer.com/2009/02/whos-this-lady-meet-selena-roberts-arods-worst-nightmare/.

13. Chris Kyle, "The Decline and Fall of Selena Roberts," Huffington Post, updated May 25, 2011, http://www.huffingtonpost.com/chris-kyle/the-decline-and-fall-of-s_b_196747.html.

14. Jason Whitlock, "Selena Roberts Reminds Me of Al Sharpton," Real Clear Sports, May 5, 2009, http://www.realclearsports.com/2009/05/06/selena_roberts_reminds_me_of_al_sharpton_59654.html.

15. John Rocker, "What If Jameis Winston Were a White Lacrosse Player?," WND.com, December 2, 2013, http://www.wnd.com/2013/12/what-if-jameis-winston-were-a-white-lacrosse-player/.

16. Travis Waldron, "ESPN Delivers Powerful Segment on Sexual Assault during Jameis Winston Coverage," *ThinkProgress*, December 6, 2013, http://thinkprogress.org/sports/2013/12/06/3029761/did-espn-cover-end-jameis-winston-case/.

17. Ibid.

18. Johnson, "The Sports Reporters," *Durham-in-Wonderland* (blog), March 5, 2007, http://durhamwonderland.blogspot.com/2007/03/sports-reporters.html.

19. "Duke Lax Players Staring Down Tough Trial—SI.com," excerpt from *Sports Illustrated* story on Newsgroups.Derkeiler.com, posted April 22, 2006, http://newsgroups.derkeiler.com/Archive/Alt/alt.true-crime/2006-04/msg04637.html.

20. Ibid.

21. Ibid.

22. "Breaking News in Search for Darren Mack," transcript of June 22, 2006, episode of *Nancy Grace*, CNN.com, http://transcripts.cnn.com/TRANSCRIPTS/0606/22/ng.01.html.

23. Associated Press, "North Carolina Governor Signs Open Discovery Bill into Law," Death Penalty Information Center, August 4, 2004, http://www.deathpenaltyinfo.org/node/1213.

24. "Breaking News in Search for Darren Mack," transcript of June 22, 2006.

25. "Duke Lax Players Are Staring Down a Tough Trial."

26. Bomani Jones, "Duke Lacrosse Celebrated for Wrong Reasons," ESPN.com, February 26, 2007, http://sports.espn.go.com/espn/page2/story?page=jones/070226.

27. Ibid.

28. Ibid.

29. Ibid.

30. Daniel Schorn, "Duke Rape Suspects Speak Out," CBSNews.com, October 11, 2006, http://www.cbsnews.com/news/duke-rape-suspects-speak-out/3/.

31. Ibid.

32. Jones, "Duke Lacross Celebrated for Wrong Reasons."

33. Johnson, "The Sports Reporters."

34. "Committees Report on Lacrosse Team Behavior, Student Judicial Processes," news release, DukeToday, May 1, 2006, http://today. duke.edu/2006/05/twocommittees.html.

CHAPTER NINE: THE NEW RACISM

1. Chris Chase, "Seahawks Star Richard Sherman's Instant-Classic Postgame Interview with Erin Andrews," *USA Today*, January 19, 2014, http://ftw.usatoday.com/2014/01/richard-sherman-erin-andrews-interview.

2. Samer Kalaf, "Dumb People Stupid, Racist Shit about Richard Sherman," *Deadspin* (blog), January 19, 2014, http://deadspin. com/dumb-people-say-stupid-racist-shit-about-richard-sherm-1504843629.

3. Kyle Wagner, "The Word 'Thug' Was Uttered 625 Times on TV on Monday. That's A Lot," *Deadspin* (blog), January 21, 2014, http:// regressing.deadspin.com/the-word-thug-was-uttered-625-times-on-tv-yesterday-1506098319.

4. Associated Press, "Fox Fires Lyons for Racially Insensitive Comment," ESPN.com, October 15, 2006, http://sports.espn. go.com/mlb/playoffs2006/news/story?id=2625500.

5. Robert Weintraub, "Color Commentators," Slate, November 30, 2006, http://www.slate.com/articles/sports/sports_nut/2006/11/color_commentators.html.

6. Mike Penner, "Voice of His Past Haunts Hamilton," *Los Angeles Times*, August 16, 2001, http://articles.latimes.com/2001/aug/16/ sports/sp-34851.

7. Ibid.

8. Weintraub, "Color Commentators."

9. John Hawkins, "The Best Quotations from Greg Gutfeld's 'The Joy of Hate,'" RightWingNews.com, May 19, 2014, http://www.

rightwingnews.com/quotes/the-best-quotations-from-greg-gutfelds-the-joy-of-hate/.

10. Max Olson, "Red McCombs Bashes Texas Hire," ESPN.com, January 8, 2014, http://espn.go.com/college-football/story/_/id/10257706/booster-red-mccombs-bashes-texas-longhorns-charlie-strong-hire.

11. Olson, "Red McCombs Bashes Texas Hire."

12. Buck Harvey, "McCombs and His Giant Mess," *My SA* (blog), January 7, 2014, http://blog.mysanantonio.com/buckharvey/2014/01/mccombs-and-his-giant-mess/.

13. Brooks, "Deion Disputes Wilbon Claim of Shanahan Racism," SportsbyBrooks.com, November 12, 2010, http://www.sportsbybrooks.com/deion-debunks-wilbon-claim-of-shanahan-racism-29234.

14. Ibid.

15. Ibid.

16. Ibid.

17. Nick Schwartz, "Eagles Receiver Riley Cooper Uses Racial Slur at a Kenny Chesney Concert," *USA Today*, July 31, 2013, http://ftw.usatoday.com/2013/07/eagles-receiver-riley-cooper-uses-racial-slur-at-a-kenny-chesney-concert.

18. Mike Florio, "Philly Mayor Says Fining Riley Cooper Isn't Good Enough," ProFootballTalk.com, August 2, 2013, http://profootballtalk.nbcsports.com/2013/08/02/philly-mayor-says-fining-riley-cooper-isnt-good-enough/.

19. Ibid.

20. Frank Schwab, "LeSean McCoy Says He Lost a Friend in Riley Cooper: 'Can't Really Respect Somebody Like That,'" Yahoo! Sports, August 1, 2013, http://sports.yahoo.com/blogs/nfl-

shutdown-corner/lesean-mccoy-says-lost-friend-riley-cooper-t-200733255.html.

21. Michael Wilbon, "Vick Owes His Second Chance to Those Willing to Give Him One," *Washington Post*, August 15, 2009, http://www.washingtonpost.com/wp-dyn/content/article/2009/08/14/AR2009081402130.html.

22. Ibid.

23. Ibid.

24. Popsspotted, "Roger Goodell Reaction to Riley Cooper Blasted as 'Gutless' and 'Unspeakably Lame' by ESPN's Michael Wilbon," *POPSspot* (blog), August 21, 2013, http://www.popsspot.com/2013/08/roger-goodell-reaction-to-riley-cooper-blasted-as-gutless-and-unspeakably-lame-by-espns-michael-wilbon/.

25. Associated Press, "Emotional Issues to Keep Dolphins T. Jonathan Martin Out for Week 9," *USA Today*, October 31, 2013, http://www.usatoday.com/story/sports/nfl/dolphins/2013/10/31/jonathan-martin-emotional-issues-out-week-9-bengals/3327929/.

26. "Richie Incognito Threatened Jonathan Martin, Used Racial Slur to Refer to Dolphins Teammate: Reports," Huffington Post, updated November 5, 2013, http://www.huffingtonpost.com/2013/11/04/richie-incognito-jonathan-martin-racial-slur-threats_n_4213340.html.

27. Ibid.

28. Ibid.

29. Breitbart Sports, "Report: Martin Threatened to Send Someone to Sodomize Incognito with 'Sandpaper Condoms,'" Breitbart Sports, Breitbart.com, January 30, 2014, http://www.breitbart.com/

Breitbart-Sports/2014/01/30/Report-Martin-Threatened-to-Send-Someone-to-Sodomize-Incognito-with-Sandpaper-Condoms.

30. Lydon Murtha, "Incognito and Martin: An Insider's Story," Monday Morning Quarterback, *Sports Illustrated*, November 7, 2013, http://mmqb.si.com/2013/11/07/richie-incognito-jonathan-martin-dolphins-lydon-murtha/.

31. Dan Graziano, "Antrel Rolle Blames Martin, Too," ESPN.com, November 7, 2013, http://espn.go.com/new-york/nfl/story/_/id/9931466/antrel-rolle-new-york-giants-says-jonathan-martin-stood-in-miami-dolphins-harassment-case.

32. Arash Markazi, "Matt Barnes: Epithet OK in Context," ESPN.com, November 15, 2013, http://espn.go.com/los-angeles/nba/story/_/id/9981526/matt-barnes-los-angeles-clippers-racial-slur-get-used-it.

33. "N-Word Controversy Is Another Example of the Liberal Takeover of American Sports," transcript from the November 18, 2013, episode of *The Rush Limbaugh Show*, http://www.rushlimbaugh.com/daily/2013/11/18/n_word_controversy_is_another_example_of_the_liberal_takeover_of_american_sports.

34. Staff, "Lil Wayne Gets Slammed for Dissing Riley Cooper for Using the N-Word," *Urban Belle*, August 4, 2013, http://urbanbellemag.com/2013/08/lil-wayne-disses-riley-cooper-blasted-for-hypocrisy.html.

35. "N-Word Controversy Is Another Example of the Liberal Takeover of American Sports."

36. Ibid.

37. Ibid.

38. Popsspotted, "Roger Goodell Reaction to Riley Cooper Blasted as 'Gutless' and 'Unspeakably Lame.'"

39. Mike Wise, "A Word You Shouldn't Use in Any Sentence," *Washington Post*, November 21, 2013, http://www.washingtonpost.com/sports/a-word-you-shouldnt-use-in-any-sentence/2013/11/21/f0e9fb38-521e-11e3-a7f0-b790929232e1_story.html.

40. Ibid.

INDEX

O

P